PERSONAL

HOW ORDINARY PEOPLE ACHIEVE

EXTRAORDINARY SUCCESS

AND HOW YOU CAN TOO

BARRY DUDDY

V

VENCAPE

PERSONAL BEST

First paperback edition printed 2012 in the United Kingdom by Vencape Publishing.

www.vencape.com

A CIP record for this book is available from the British Library.

ISBN 978-0-9574009-0-0

For more copies of this book, please email: info@vencape.com

About the Author:

Barry Duddy is an Author, Speaker, and the CEO of Personal Best Research, a personal development and business improvement consultancy. Having built his own high growth business, he now consults with individuals, companies and organisations to assist them in maximising their potential. Personal Best was founded to share the knowledge and best practice of selected achievers, companies and groups from around the world.

Find out more at: **www.personalbest.co.uk**

Thank you for buying this book. Today you have touched the life of someone in need.

Every time a copy of Personal Best is bought, someone, somewhere in the world, benefits directly through the funds raised and work done by Buy1GIVE1.

To find out more about this incredible movement that supports charities worldwide go to: www.b1g1.com

This book is dedicated to Cara Duddy and to you the reader, for investing in this book and committing to being your best.

Personal Best would not exist had it not been for the time and insights provided by a large number of contributors who agreed to share their philosophies. Although some prefer to remain anonymous, I thank them all for their input and I am indebted to those listed below, who for no other reason, than they felt that their ideas might benefit others, gave up their time and dedicated their minds to assist in building the central themes of this book.

Sir Frank Williams - Founder, Williams Grand Prix	Lord Harris – Chairman, Carpetright PLC
Sir Chris Evans – Biotech Entrepreneur	Tony Hsieh – CEO, Zappos
Sir George Buckley – Chairman, 3M	Lord Michael Ashcroft – Former Chairman, ADT
Sir Tom Farmer – Founder, Kwik Fit Group	Lord Neil Kinnock – Former Labour Leader
Dave Scott – Six times World Ironman Champion and First Hall of Fame Inductee	Tony Fernandes – CEO, Air Asia
Mike Duke – CEO Wal-Mart	Trevor Baylis OBE – Inventor
Lord Paddy Ashdown – Former Liberal Party Leader	Lynne Sedgmore – Executive Director, 157 Group
Baroness Pauline Perry	Mark Emalfarb – CEO, Dyadic
Baroness Susan Greenfield CBE – Neuroscientist	Mark Turner – CEO, OC Group
Bernie Siegel – Author and healer	Martin Dunphy – CEO, Marlin Capital

Flemming Bligaard Pedersen – CEO Ramboll & European CEO of the Year	Maureen O'Sullivan – TD, Irish Parliament
Ron G Holland – Entrepreneur & Author	Michael Meacher – MP
Bob Kaplan – Author and Professor, Harvard Business School	Sir Michael Smurfit – Chairman, Smurfit Group
Brad Feld – CEO, Foundry Group	Mike Gooley – Founder, Trailfinders PLC
Brian Bacon – CEO, Oxford Leadership	Lord Redesdale – Chairman, Carbon Management Association
Brianna Glenn – Athlete, USA	Nick Friedman – CEO, College Hunks Hauling Junk
Bruce Perlowin – Entrepreneur and CEO, Hemp Inc	Nick Jenkins – Director, Hansei Australia
Mark Allen – Six times World Ironman Champion	Nigel Dessau – Chief Marketing Officer, AMD
Cary Cooper – Singer/Songwriter	Nigel Evans – MP, Deputy Speaker
Charles Wigoder – CEO, Telecom Plus PLC	Nirmalya Kumar – Author & Professor of Marketing, London Business School
Chris Guillbeau – Author of Non Conformity & The $100 start up	Noel Grealish – TD Irish Parliament
Lord Chris Rennard – Former CEO, Liberal Party	Baron Giles Radice
Craig Sams – Founder, Green & Blacks Chocolate	Paul Dunn – Chairman, Buy1GIVE1
Dan Henry – CEO, Netspend	Paul Flynn – MP

David Alton, Lord Liverpool – Human rights campaigner and author	Paul Kehoe – Minister of Transport Ireland
John Lyons – TD, Irish Parliament	Chuck Jones – Chief Design Officer, Masco
David Novak – CEO, Yum	Rachel Elnaugh – Entrepreneur
Toni McIntosh –Scottish Marathon Champion	Robert Edmiston – Chairman, IM Group
Deborah Myer – CMO, Pulte Group	Roger Smith – CEO, OBN Holdings
Doug Baird – CEO, Interim Partners	Ron Hill – Olympian and former Marathon world record holder
Dr. Gerard Lyons – Chief Economist, Standard Chartered Bank	Shama Kabani – CEO Marketing Zen
Finian McGrath – TD, Irish Parliament	Simon Clifford – Founder, Brazilian Soccer Schools
Frank McKinney – Bestselling author and real estate rockstar	Simon Tucker – CEO, SRT PLC
Indro Mukerjee – CEO, Plastic Logic	Alan Edwards – CEO, Outside Organisation
Prof Henry Mintzberg – Author and management thinker	Ali Lukies – CEO, Monitise PLC
Jim Fleeting – Director, Scottish Football Association	Anne Handley – Founder, Marketing Profs
Joasia Zakrzewski – Ultra runner and World Medallist	Christian Bergmann – CEO Alegro Capital
John Adair – Chair, United Nations Strategic Leadership	Zac Johnson – Affiliate Marketing Expert

Errol Kerr – Olympic Skier	Tom Chapman – Founder, Matches Fashion
Julian Richer – CEO, Richer Sounds	Lord Robin Butler
Carl Elsener – CEO, Victorinix	Lord Mackay – Former Lord Chancellor
Ken Maginnis, Lord Drumglass	Lord Selkirk
Charlotte Bray – Composer	Viscount Ellis
Lord Adam Patel – Entrepreneur	Dennis Skinner – MP
Lord Brian McKenzie	Abhishek Rungta – CEO, Indus Net Technologies
Lord Eric Avebury	Jez Cox – Performance Consultant & Team GB Duathlon Manager
Dame Fiona Reynolds - Master of Emmanuel College, Cambridge	Jim Alder – Former Commonwealth Marathon Champion
John Redwood – MP, former Secretary of State for Wales	Helen Bamber, OBE – Psychotherapist
Teresa Amabile – Author & Professor of Business Harvard Business School	Olympia Scott – Professional Basketball Player & CEO Super Parenting
David Meerman Scott – Author and CEO, Freshspot	Pete Cowen – Golf Coach to Darren Clarke, Lee Westwood and Padraig Harrington
B. K. S. Iyengar – Founder, Iyengar Yoga	Dean Finch – CEO National Express
Joseph Wan – CEO, Harvey Nichols	Peter Bieler – CEO Media Funding & Infomercial Pioneer

Contents:

Part One: PERSONAL

A commitment to being your best.

The power of purpose and the two most important questions you will ever ask.

How passion and energy drive your dreams.

Developing irresistible momentum and courage.

Identifying your niche and becoming an expert authority.

Part Two: BEST

Foreword:

Sir Frank Williams - Founder & Team Principal, Williams Formula One Racing.

From my school days I was always fascinated by motor racing. I then found myself gravitating more towards watching motor racing trackside, I met other itinerant racing drivers, all foreigners (at that time England was the source of nearly all motor racing equipment), so I was being continuously asked, I'm happy to say, can you get me this, can you get me that? Which I did, and brought back to the various continental races. A little business grew and eventually I thought I could do this for a long time, make money and enter Formula 2 myself, which I did and this then became Formula 1.

As for the motivation? It just happens. Anyone in racing will tell you the same thing, when you're a racer, you want to race. It's not a conceited remark in anyway, there's no turning back because there's nothing else I'd want to do it is the same for many people working at Williams. It's a wonderful human gift, which I'm exploiting! Speaking for myself, I just love Formula 1, I love motor racing, love cars, love speed. I still love speed. It's just a thing you don't have to think about it.

The most valuable and clever advice I've been given was given to me in my youth and of course as you have probably been told by your father, when you're young you think you know everything and think you know best and it was the same with me – I learned by my mistakes and if I was being fair and honest I'd say I had very good mentors along the way. I must say, operating in Formula 1 you come across some formidable individuals, people who are very clever, who are commercially very astute; Mr Ecclestone is the best example, very clever people and if you have brains yourself you'll learn from them.

The purpose of the sport is to be the best that you can be and to beat everybody. What goes along with that of course is sometimes people are just a little bit better than you are and that is called competition. Formula 1 is a competitive sport and a competitive business. All you can do is your best each day.

Frank Williams

Sir Frank Williams has led Williams Grand Prix to nine F1 Constructors Championships, seven Drivers Championships and more than one hundred Grand Prix race victories.

Introduction:

Sir Tom Farmer – Founder Kwik Fit Group

To succeed in business, you must have enthusiasm, you must have energy and it has to be an obsession, a magnificent obsession, an inner passion of your being.

The main thing stopping people is themselves, it is simple as that; there are opportunities out there. You have to be sure you have a product and service that people want, but there are opportunities out there every day of the week and if you have the ability, the self-motivation and if you have done your homework beforehand, you will be able to give the time and energy that's required.

I often remind people that business isn't about computers, it isn't about fancy advertising programmes or premises, it all is about people, the relationships with the people in your organisation, the relationships with your suppliers, relationships with your customers, you have to make sure that interpersonal relationships are right: it helps to overcome any problem that may arise. So surround yourself with likeminded people, those people whose company you enjoy and with whom you can build great relationships, by doing this you will have great success. That's how you can become your best.

Sir Tom Farmer

PART ONE: **PERSONAL**

CHAPTER 1: **Personal Best**

Faith is taking the first step even when you don't see the whole staircase. - Martin Luther King, Jr.

Those who achieve great things in their lives are not superhuman. They are not genetically superior and their backgrounds do not predict what they might accomplish. They do, however, share a similar mindset and follow similar disciplines. Success leaves clues and Personal Best is focused on identifying those traits and providing a blueprint to help anyone make improvements in any area of their life.

This book has been written with the help of over two hundred people who agreed to be interviewed or who shared their thoughts, key quotes from these achievers can be found throughout this book. Personal Best is intended to show not only the primary factors in the accomplishments of people who have achieved outstanding success in their lives, but also to provide a roadmap to allow you to realise your own goals. That is the principle of this book. Regardless of where you are in your life, no matter what you might want to achieve, by committing to be your best and following the guidance provided by more than two hundred successful people, you have a bulletproof methodology to realise massive and lasting improvements. People who achieve things consistently are not that different from you, they just have a different strategy. The first part of this book covers those essential traits and the second part provides direct and proven methods that you can use to make leaps forward in your life.

Success means different things to different people; it also means something different to each of us as we move through life. Goals, values and aspirations can change, but whatever success means to you – be it personal, financial, spiritual, related to your career, improving your relationships, enhancing your health or all of these things – this book has been written as a guide as to what works. It shows what achievers from a wide range of backgrounds do consistently to realise their aims, and provides tools that allow you to duplicate their habits to progress in your own life.

Personal Best can be used as a guide to become the very best that you can be in any way that you might imagine.

The Personal Best ethos is based around doing what an athlete would do to achieve a personal best time on the track. Rarely does anyone from the world of athletics improve by twenty per cent overnight. An athlete commits to working to a set training plan, so that over a period of time ongoing improvements will be made. The way that athletes improve is by doing a little bit more every day, by stretching themselves in each session. The most incredible thing is that when you work to a focused goal-orientated plan, even though the changes you make seem relatively minor on a daily basis, the overall gains are incredible. They can happen quickly, building momentum for more gains. Anyone who has children can relate to the massive steps they take without us really noticing. When we meet someone who has not seen our family for a while, they tend to comment on how much the children have grown or matured and we have not noticed because we see our kids every day. Their progress is gradual, so we are less aware of their development.

Personal Best People: Joseph Wan - Chief Executive, Harvey Nichols
"Just because you are born gifted or talented, that doesn't mean that good things will just come to you. Nothing will be given to you or fall to you from heaven. You have to work hard if you are to realise your full potential. Today I am giving that same advice to my own children."

When I began my journey of interviewing some of the most successful people in the world, I was keen to bring together the common threads of knowledge and habits they shared. The main theme that I found in their stories (and something that anyone can immediately duplicate), is that they ask a little more of themselves consistently. They push a little more, stretching beyond what they had done previously. I found this to be true in business, politics, spiritual leadership and financial achievement. They simply took responsibility, not only for themselves and their own actions, but also when handling challenges and situations outside their direct control.

The contrast in the ability of some people to overcome difficult circumstances when others cannot was shown starkly to me the day I met former Police Chief Superintendent and policy advisor to the Government, Brian Mackenzie. He serves as a working peer in the House of Lords and in this role he has the influence to help shape legislation that will become law. I was keen to track his career and in particular to find out why he has worked so hard to change certain elements of the statute book. Brian is proud of having shaped several key areas of legislation and in particular the change in the law relating to double jeopardy. This was the law that meant a person could not be tried twice for the same crime, even if new evidence came to light. Brian was a passionate advocate for the abolition of this law, which he saw as a persistent barrier to justice.

Brian told me that this had been on his mind ever since he served as a young police officer in Durham, at the time a man called Donald Hume had escaped justice for the murder of a business associate. He was tried for the killing but there was not enough evidence to secure a conviction and he was acquitted of murder. Hume subsequently admitted the crime and sold his story to a Sunday newspaper, describing in graphic detail how he had killed, dismembered and disposed of his victim. Given that he had already been tried, the law could not touch him. Hume then went on to kill a taxi driver in Switzerland some years later. The injustice of this stayed with Brian, so much so that years later he became the driving force behind the change in this law. That afternoon I had some downtime between interviews, so I did some research on Hume's background.

DONALD

Donald Hume endured a terrible childhood; this does not excuse his future heinous acts, but perhaps explains the psyche of such an individual. Hume was abandoned by his mother soon after birth and was sent to an orphanage. The institution he ended up in was bleak and no compassion was shown to the young residents within it. They were regarded as the sons and daughters of sinners and treated accordingly. Beatings and punishments were commonplace and the owners even kept a parrot that shouted out the word 'bastard', just to remind the children of what they were. The orphanage set the tone for the hatred that Hume would later admit to feeling towards the world. When, at the age of seven, Hume lifted an axe and attempted to attack a member of staff who was teasing him, he was transferred to live with an aunt. Life did not improve much over the next few years as his aunt indulged her daughters and treated him with coldness and contempt. Donald Hume's hatred was compounded when he discovered that his 'aunt' was in fact his birth mother, who had abandoned him and did not now want to acknowledge him as her own.

Hume left home as soon as he could and lived a life of petty crime and larceny, culminating in his becoming a double murderer.

This is not a pleasant story and inevitably we will speculate on how his adult life might have differed had he enjoyed a happy childhood.

GEORGE

I moved on to my next interview with a genial man in his sixties called George. He too had been abandoned at a young age. His mother had given birth to him just after the war and soon after she handed him to his grandmother who ran a boarding house in Sheffield. He was brought up in grinding poverty with several of his brothers and sisters. Of the five of them, only George and one sister lived beyond childhood. Chillingly, in later years George's sister checked the death certificates of their siblings, which may imply that infanticide could have been the cause of their deaths. No charges were ever laid: such was life in the most poverty stricken areas of post-war Britain.

When he was still a toddler, George's grandmother offered him to a travelling family who had happened to stay in her house for a few nights; George was given to these strangers and separated from his brothers and sisters. The family George lived with were kind to him, but the reality of their life was also one of harsh poverty and George's life was itinerant and directionless. At the age of five he was enrolled in school, but he had kidney problems and also suffered from anaemia and chronic bronchitis, due in no small part to the penurious existence that he lived. These physical afflictions meant that he was not permitted to attend the local school (in those days any affliction could lead to segregation as a no-hoper and being sent to a special school for such cases). George therefore had a limited education and his tumultuous life became more complex when a woman claiming to be his mother demanded that the family he lived with hand him back. They duly did so and despite not even recognising his mother, having been away from her virtually since birth, George moved to a new home with her and the man she now lived with, who became his stepfather. But his mother soon left again, leaving George with his stepfather and stepbrother. From the age of eight George pretty much fended for himself as his stepdad was either working or looking for work. This lonely, impoverished life became worse when George's stepbrother began to sexually assault him and he was regularly attacked by the older boy. George became adept at keeping an escape route available at all times when he was in the house, and he took to wandering the streets rather than risk further attacks by staying at home.

At the age of fifteen George left school with no qualifications. He secured an apprenticeship as an electrical engineer and he has an abiding memory of the man he was working with attempting to explain circuitry and the basic workings of electricity to him. George was stupefied. He simply could not comprehend what he was being told.

Personal Best People: George Buckley - Chairman and CEO 3M
"In life I decided that I could be a victim or a victor. I chose the latter."

At this stage in his life, George had every right to hate the world and everyone in it. He had been born into poverty and had been passed from home to home throughout his childhood. He had suffered chronic illness, been denied a full education and had been subject to the most unspeakable assaults. He had no qualifications and had received no guidance. All he had was a belief that he held. George told me, 'In life I decided that I could be a victim or a victor. I chose the latter'.

The teenage George enrolled at a College of Further Education and studied there part-time for several years while learning his trade during the day. He then went on to university where he gained a doctorate in electrical engineering and secured a management position with British Rail. Eventually George moved to the United States, after being offered a senior role with Emerson Electric, and in 2005 he took over at the industrial giant 3M as Chairman and CEO. Under Buckley's stewardship the business has enjoyed sustained revenue and profit growth, with annual revenues of over $26 billion. George is now regarded as one of the world's top business leaders, and needless to say he has been well rewarded for his stellar contribution. He was knighted in 2011 for his services to business.

Two very different stories. Why is it that two people can experience similar circumstances yet respond in different ways? Why is it that Donald Hume and George Buckley both grew up through frightening and horrific childhoods, but one grew up to be double murderer, and the other to be an extraordinarily successful businessman? The reasons for this will become clear as you read through this book, but the primary reason lies in the thinking and mental processing that each undertook.

Why positive thinking isn't enough:

You may at some point have read a book or gone to a seminar that promoted positive thinking as a cure-all to bring happiness, joy and fulfilment into your life. These seminars have merit and I believe anyone can benefit from building positive expectation as a habitual way of thinking; however, this is only half the story. Positive thinking without concerted intelligent action can lead to frustration and disillusionment. Positive thoughts are powerful but can undermine the best-laid plans.

I live near the coast. It is a truly beautiful area and somewhere I am glad to call home. However, in my part of the world, it rains, frequently, and in different ways. Heavy rain, light rain, drizzle, sweeping-in-from-the-side rain, spitting rain and so on. Now, I could repeat incantations that focus on the fact that it will not rain. I can repeatedly visualise that every day will be warm and sunny and that I will enjoy nothing but pleasant weather. This will not change the meteorological fact that it rains around one hundred and sixty days a year here. If I have any sense, I know I had better wear a jacket, carry an umbrella and enjoy my day.

In life, it is the same; we do not have to throw our intelligence out of the window. We can retain a positive expectation but still be ready to handle the showers if they come. Our thinking will dictate what and who we become, so I am all for keeping that positive mindset, without losing sight of the fact that I share the world with billions of others, who may be thinking or desiring something else. Blinkered thinking which says things will always turn out exactly as we want them to or that we will win the prize and everyone else will lose is not only limiting, but self-defeating. This attitude can still be found in individuals, organisations and companies. I admire the sheer force of desire to make something happen, but if two people or companies are chasing the same thing, who wins? If there can only be one number one, whose positive thinking is more powerful? Personal Best gives you an intelligent way of enjoying fast progress, by employing the tools used by everyone who has achieved notable success. Without pushing aside your native intelligence, it allows you to keep running towards all the things you want in life and to do so with balance and integrity.

THE TORPEDO

Richard Thompson realised that he was a quick runner when he was about eight years old. He found himself able to beat kids much older than him as they raced across the school yard in his home town of Cascade in Trinidad and Tobago. He used this speed to great effect on the football field, becoming an accomplished player with a turn of pace that left defenders in his wake. As he got older, Richard decided to concentrate on track and field rather than football. He won a number of races during his college years and was disappointed not to qualify for the Trinidad and Tobago national team during the 2005 Central American Games in Nassau. However, by working with an experienced coach and dedicating himself to his training, he eventually improved his 100 metre time from 10.47 seconds in 2005 to 10.09 in 2007. His performances were good enough for selection into the team that travelled to the World Athletics Championships in Osaka, Japan that summer. Richard qualified from his first heat, but did not manage to get past the second round where he finished last of the eight runners chasing the qualifying places for the final. His mood was upbeat though; he was getting faster and was still only twenty-two. At his age he still had time to mature and get stronger. In fact many sprinters still perform superbly well in their thirties.

Richard's main goal was to qualify for the team that would travel to the Olympic Games a year later in Beijing. After a good winter season, including a new personal best over 60 metres at an indoor event, his 2008 place on the Olympic team was confirmed and he travelled to participate in the 100 metres, where he would be pitted against the best in the world. After the previous year's effort, Richard was determined to make the final eight, although this was a difficult task, given the calibre of the athletes he would be up against. But he was running well and his confidence was high; he believed himself capable of making the Olympic final, which would be an achievement beyond that which many commentators expected. Richard won his first heat and qualified for the quarter finals. He knew that he would have to run to the top of his ability now as he was lined up against other world class sprinters who had come through their heats, including Tyson Gay, the American champion. Richard breezed through in an astonishing 9.99 seconds. He was delighted. Rarely do athletes peak at exactly the right time, but he had. He was running strongly and felt he might have a little more in him. He was in the semi-finals, one race away from his goal and a place in the final of the Olympic Games.

When the gun went in his semi-final heat, Richard got out of the blocks beautifully, quickly hit his stride and pushed through halfway strongly. He powered through the last fifty metres to finish second behind renowned Jamaican sprinter Asafa Powell in a new personal best time of 9.93 seconds. Incredibly he had done it; by pulling out the performance of his life he had not only qualified for the Olympic final but had also achieved a time that even he had doubted he was capable of. No one can ask more of themselves than to push further than they have ever done previously. Not everyone can be top of the class or become President, or win the gold medal, but by taking massive, intelligent action we are all capable of achieving things that might seem beyond our current abilities.

The Olympic final of 2008 was much anticipated and as it turned out it was an historic event. The world's greatest sprinter Usain Bolt powered down the track in a breathtaking 9.69 seconds. Even by the high standards Bolt had set himself this seemed almost superhuman. The distance between him and the rest of the field was large and still growing as he started celebrating his victory ten metres before the finish line. It was incredible to witness an athlete smashing the world record in such a seemingly effortless style. What about Richard? Well, he scored yet another massive personal best, flying down the track in 9.89 seconds. He not only achieved another PB, his second in as many days, but he also secured the silver medal and became a national hero in his homeland.

Should Richard celebrate his incredible achievement or should he be disappointed that he finished second? Should he look at his progress and the huge accomplishment of running faster than he had ever done in his life, or be down because he had finished behind the fastest man on the planet? This is what Richard said in an interview immediately after the race. "Words cannot describe how I feel right now. This is just a dream come true for me. I have to tip my hat to Usain Bolt; he's a great competitor, a phenomenal athlete, and there was no way anyone was going to beat him with a run like that. But it just feels good to come here, run in the Olympic Games, my first Olympic Games, win a silver medal and run a personal best at the same time. I couldn't ask for anything more, thank God."

The ethos of Personal Best:

Your life is about private and personal victories. Maybe you don't go home with a gold medal, but if you do more than you ever thought possible, you have made progress and gained pride in the personal success of having done something you had never achieved before. If you can do a bit more, be it in the workplace, or within the home, if you strive just to be better than you were before, your life will open up and you will progress more than you could ever imagine. This commitment to ongoing improvement can be the cornerstone to incredible achievement. When you set a goal and move towards it by taking daily actions focused on its attainment, then you are working to a Personal Best ethos. If you have a clear target and you take ongoing, relentless action – constantly improving yourself, constantly asking more of yourself – then you will undoubtedly achieve your goals, faster and more effectively than you ever thought possible.

Personal Best People: Sir Frank Williams - Founder Williams Grand Prix

"The purpose of the sport is to be the best that you can be and to beat everybody. What goes along with that of course is sometimes people are just a little bit better than you are and that is called competition. Formula 1 is a competitive sport and a competitive business."

There is not one person of note that I interviewed who didn't admit to stretching themselves at some point in their lives and usually on an ongoing basis. They consistently did that which they hadn't done before. Often they had no frame of reference, having had no previous experience or any reason to believe they could conceivably achieve their goal. They just decided on what they wanted, and the way they achieved it was by a process of ongoing improvement. We know this makes sense in all fields of endeavour. In sports you might struggle to run to the end of your street, but if every day you try to go fifty yards further than the previous day, then day by day, week by week, you will build your strength. In short order you will be running for miles. You will be capable of doing a marathon. There is no secret behind it. It is just a case of doing a little more every day.

The Personal Best method is simply a commitment to ongoing improvement and it is a quality that I found in everybody I spoke to. What keeps a sportsperson motivated? Once they have won everything they can, why do they keep going? Once somebody becomes a millionaire or even a billionaire, what drives them forward? Once somebody has written a scientific paper that changes the world, why do they keep going to work? The reason can be found in the deep-rooted sense of purpose that such people have and also in the love of what they do. They have an absolute unending commitment to being the best they can be. They want to stretch themselves and ask more of themselves. They want to find out what they are capable of, to discover what more they can achieve. That is what makes the difference. It is behind every great story and behind every success that I found during my research. Great people don't become great by accident. They just ask a little bit more of themselves.

Setting the standard:

This is what is truly exciting. If one person can do something, then so can you. If you follow the same methodologies as someone who excels in their field, you will also succeed. The key distinction between people who seemingly come from nowhere to outstanding achievement is that they set higher standards. Admittedly there are key drivers and strategies that they employ (which will be outlined as you continue reading), but these can be duplicated. Fundamentally the question to ask of yourself is: are you willing to set yourself a higher standard and commit yourself to achieving it? This doesn't mean having to make a quantum leap overnight. It simply means consistently making small improvements to relevant areas of your life, be it business, finance, fitness, health, family or relationships. If you just try to become a little bit better at what you do each and every day, then the success you will experience will astonish you. Once you decide that you will be your best and you take appropriate daily actions, you will look back on each day and see that you have attained more than you ever have before. Do this every day and you will have a good week. Do this every week and you will have a good month. Every year you will take strides towards the greatest dreams of your life. And when you look back on the tapestry of your life, it will be one of achievement and fulfilment.

The way to attain anything you want in life can be summed up in a simple way. Decide the price that needs to be paid and pay the price. Achieving each goal may not be easy, but it is simple. It might mean pushing yourself when you would rather take the day off. It might mean working harder. It might mean developing more understanding. Whatever it means, if it takes you to where you want to go, it is a price worth paying.

The people I spoke to during my research came from all walks of life, but the one thing they had in common was an absolute commitment to continuous improvement. Whether consciously or subconsciously, they just became better at what they did over a period of years. They continually asked more of themselves and consequently achieved their aims.

Becoming better at something doesn't have to be painful but it does have to be consistent.

Personal Best is centred on giving you an intelligent plan to help drive you towards your personal goals. Nothing in life feels as good as knowing you are getting better. It is such a fundamental need for all of us; it is what keeps people going. If you know that you are expanding your horizons, if you feel that you are getting better every day, it is life-enhancing. It is the essence of life.

Personal Best People: Baroness Pauline Perry - Former Chief Inspector of Schools and first woman to run a British University
"Ambition is not a bad thing."

As humans, we have excelled due to our self-awareness and consciousness. We have always looked to improve ourselves and our environment; both as individuals and within societies we look to develop and move forward. Our progression as a species has been incredible over many thousands of years. In more recent times, technology has constantly pushed the boundaries of our knowledge, of our medical capabilities and of virtually any area that we care to think about. We are living in contradiction to our values if we do not work towards being our personal best each and every day. Taking progressive action is the only way that we can improve. If we act strongly, wilfully and consistently, our actions will become habitual. If we want to experience joy in our lives, we have to be sure that we are constantly improving. It is when things stay still or when we think that we are not making progress that we become frustrated. Something I feel sure you will agree with is that the world around us is constantly changing. The corollary to this, which we sometimes miss, is that we have to be constantly changing with it. Better still, we have to be constantly improving. Believe me, we are not standing on the side of the hill. We are either marching up it or we are sliding down. If we put a thousand pounds in the bank and go back a year later, the thousand pounds will still be there but it will have less value. If nothing else, inflation will take a chunk out of it. So it is with our lives. We are either moving forward or sliding backwards. There is no stationary point.

When people talk about someone's overnight success, they don't always see the commitment; they don't see the ongoing improvements that were made in that person's life. They just see the success, and that person coming from nowhere into the public consciousness. But we are all intelligent enough to know that there is always a story behind the story. There are the unheralded moments in that person's life when he or she pushed a little harder, invested more time, became dedicated to improving skills and committed to being their best. Sometimes people look at that type of individual and say, "Look how lucky they are." But as the Roman philosopher Seneca said "Luck is what happens when preparation meets opportunity."

Raising the Bar:

Personal Best People: Sir Tom Farmer - Founder Kwik Fit Group
"The main thing stopping you is yourself. I am absolutely serious about that.
There are opportunities out there. You just have to go and find them."

I believe passionately that you should set incredible, mind-expanding goals and that you should paint vistas for your life that perhaps don't seem believable. If you have a big enough reason to achieve what you want, you will find a way to achieve it. However, one of the issues which many people have when they set goals or when they set out to achieve something, is that their objectives seem so far away. The journey of a thousand miles may well begin with the first step, but a thousand miles is still a hell of a long way. So people set out with good intentions but they set such a lofty, ambitious goal that they become overwhelmed by it. The initial excitement of setting their aim can dissipate quickly when they come to terms with the magnitude of what has to be done to achieve it.

The other challenge which people face when setting major goals is that they simply don't believe them. They may well set out to achieve their aims, but a small voice in their head tells them they are trying to achieve something that is beyond their reach. Consequently they wonder whether it is worth even starting on the journey towards their goal.

Personal Best People: Ronald Kers - CEO Muller Dairies
"Since the age of 28, I have always had clear goals and milestones planned for my personal life in terms of what I want to achieve. This included areas like professional, family, society, friends, and purely "me". I have tried to stick to these milestones and so far I have to say that most of what I planned, especially in terms of professional and family I have accomplished either ahead of time or on time and to the level I expected."

The fantastic thing about committing to be your personal best is that all you have to do is just get a little better in the areas relevant to your goals. If you are going to start that business then all you need to do every day is to take small steps towards realising that dream. If you are going to write that book, then commit to writing as many words as you can each day. These things are believable. Simple acts that you can complete comfortably will bring you closer each day to your ultimate goal. Taking these important, incremental steps means that before long you may well have created the next breakthrough business or written the next great novel. Who knows where it can take you?

So, set ambitious goals, but commit yourself to smaller actionable steps. What small actions can you take that will move you towards your goals? What knowledge can you gain each and every day that will get you there? What information do you need and where will you find it? All you need to do is day by day, week by week take steps towards what you want to achieve in life. This is maybe the most important promise you will ever make. A promise to ongoing improvement, a commitment to being your best is what will make the difference in your life. Opportunities and happenstance start moving in your favour and you will begin noticing that you are simply becoming better at what you do.

So let's move forward. What are the key qualities that successful people have used to attain fantastic results? There are many traits that the very best shared with me. In outlining them here, we can look to elicit these core strategies, and having done this we can build a system, a way of acting that will deliver us the same results.

How it fits together:

Throughout the book you will see Personal Best quotes from those who committed their time and gave vital insights as to which habits and strategies work for them. The themes common to virtually everyone I spoke to, studied and interviewed are covered in the first part of this book, which I have labelled PERSONAL:

Purpose

Enthusiasm

Resilience

Specialise

Ongoing improvement

Nerve

Action

Leadership

Every one of the achievers I spent time with was driven by a **purpose**, somewhat larger than their own ego or self-interest. They had an **enthusiasm** and passion for their subject matter and had shown **resilience** when circumstance turned against them. They were all **specialised** and skilled in their area of expertise – but don't confuse skill with talent. We will look at this area and the strength of practise over natural ability. All were committed to the process of **ongoing improvement** and showed **nerve**; that is to say they faced their fears when they found themselves in difficult situations; they had the courage to take the necessary **actions** to stay the course. Finally they were all **leaders**, although not exclusively in the traditional sense of leading others; they excelled in leading themselves, through self-discipline and personal integrity. They demanded more of themselves than anyone else could reasonably have done.

The second part of this book, which I have labelled BEST, shows the key tools we can use to make giant steps in our own lives.

Belief

Emulate

Strategy

Thinking

If you employ these methods, they will allow you to shortcut years of learning, by tapping into the mindset and the thinking patterns of the very best that have gone before you. In this section, we will look at the power of **beliefs**, the core beliefs which you have to either catapult you forward or hold you back. We will study how the best usually got that way by **emulating** someone else's success; to some degree they either modelled themselves on someone, or a key person made a huge impact on their lives. You will also require a **strategy**, a means of putting into place a compelling life plan to drive you forward. Finally, we will examine your capacity for **thinking**; what your mental state is, day in and day out, and how this can be altered to make you a different person.

Throughout the book I'll ask some questions of you. To start your journey all you need do is grab a pen and note down your answers to these questions. Make that promise to yourself now. If you have ever not followed through or fallen short of what you could be, decide now that you will do one thing. As well as reading the information in this book, you will act on it by thinking about these questions. It is a small commitment and if you take the time to consider these questions, you will start to tap in to your own most vital resource, your mind, and become closer to achieving a new way of living, of being your best.

Let's begin by looking at the biggest driver of success throughout time immemorial. The one that every single person I spoke to has a huge sense of and feeling for.

Purpose.

CHAPTER 2: **Purpose**

Many people have a wrong idea of what constitutes true happiness. It is not attained through self-gratification, but through fidelity to a worthy purpose. - Helen Keller

Each of us has a purpose in life. In Indian culture there is a beautiful word for it – *dharma* – which simply means your true calling in life. But many people live their life focused on things that are not in harmony with their true values. They live to a script that they believe has to be worked to. These choices are often based on beliefs related to income requirement, family demands, what their parents did or what their teachers thought.

Before you can begin any journey you have to know where you are going. You must be sure of what you want and you have to ask yourself, 'Does this lead me to my purpose in life?' It's a question we rarely ask ourselves. What do you really want to achieve? What do you really want to do? If you ask yourself this question, with heartfelt intent, you should come up with some powerful answers that will give you a platform to design a life of abundance.

Personal Best People: Rachel Elnaugh - Entrepreneur
"You have to have a definite chief aim."

All the hard work, diligence, qualifications and determination in the world will count for nothing unless you have identified what you want your life to become. To do this, all you need do is answer two simple questions – the two most important questions you will ever ask yourself. Take the time right now to answer them.

What do you want?

Why do you want it?

Reflect on these questions or better still ask them of yourself every day of your life, because the quality of your life is going to be decided by those two questions. The key thing that will allow you to make life-changing decisions is the quality of the questions that you ask yourself. If you will commit to asking yourself intelligent questions, you will come up with intelligent answers that will point the way towards improving your life experience.

Your questions are your answers:

Personal Best People: Nirmalya Kumar - Author and Professor of Marketing at London Business School.
"The most valuable advice I have received is always think about the next question to answer."

Your mind is programmed to answer thousands of questions every day. What shall I have for lunch? What was that noise? Who was meant to collect the kids from school? How will I finish this report? What is the square root of pi? The list goes on. Your mind is incredibly powerful when it comes to answering questions ranging from the highly complex to the mundane. What it does not do, however, is ascertain the quality of the question. If you ask, 'Why am I rubbish at this?' or 'Why am I so fat? Your brain is wired to come back with direct answers. So your mind may well tell you that you are rubbish at something because you are stupid, or that you are fat because you are a greedy sloth. It is much more productive to ask yourself more empowering questions, such as; 'How can I get better at this?' or 'How can I get into shape?' because then your brain will come back with empowering answers. These could tell you where you could obtain the information to increase your competencies, or tell you what steps you could take to obtain the physical wellbeing you desire.

This is a fairly simplistic overview of the incredible processor that is the human mind and one that we will explore more fully as we move through this book. However, the point about the questions you ask yourself is important and it is something that you can start doing right now because in every given moment, the quality of your life will be driven by the quality of the questions that you ask yourself. Let me remind you once more.

The quality of your life will be driven by the quality of the questions that you ask yourself and you will never ask yourself anything more important than 'What do I want?' and 'Why do I want it?'

Sometimes these questions seem almost too big to answer at one sitting. Designing your life can be a daunting process when you are preoccupied with your everyday activities. Deciding your chief aim in life can seem overwhelming, indeed it may be that whatever you decide to do may not seem important to anyone other than yourself. That's OK. We cannot all be the person that cures cancer or leads our country, but in our own way we can all make a positive impact on the world.

PAUL'S PURPOSE

I try to attend new seminars, meetings and network events whenever possible. I think it widens both my knowledge and contact base. However, when a business colleague suggested that we go to hear a marketing speaker who was going to be in Glasgow, I was reluctant. It was a busy week, I had a lot of commitments and the last thing I needed was to spend a morning in a room, listening to someone deliver a talk, no matter how well intentioned that might be.

Eventually, I agreed to go along and I am glad I did. Not only did I learn a bit more about the speaker and his world view, but his talk also made me stop and evaluate my own life's purpose. The speaker was a man called Paul Dunn, an engineer by training. He was one of the first employees of Hewlett Packard when it was launched in Australia. Paul rose up the ranks through a variety of engineering positions before deciding that his real passion was for marketing. He worked in this area for Hewlett Packard for several years, helping to position the company as a premium solutions provider throughout Australia and Asia. In 1980, Paul decided that he wanted to paddle his own canoe and so he started his own company, The Results Corporation, which provided outsourced marketing services. Over the next fifteen years Paul built the business into a twenty million dollar company, serving small and new enterprises throughout the world.

As Paul talked about his career and life, it was clear that he had a deep knowledge and understanding of his area of expertise. He was smart, engaging and clearly qualified to talk about marketing. He provided intelligent insights into what really worked and how to build a base of loyal customers. All of this was interesting, but my day wasn't getting any less busy. From time to time I glanced at my phone

45

and saw the email list building up with enquiries and questions from my clients. With many of the seminars that I attend, the speakers tend to build up towards the end of the presentation. Effectively they try to convince you they are worth listening to, give you some worthwhile information, and then suggest that you purchase their book, audio programme or sign up for a four day seminar, where they can give you some really valuable insights. There is nothing wrong with this. If someone can deliver value they have every right to bang their drum, but time was marching on and I felt Paul was still building up to his finale. He had another story to tell. I wished he would get on with it and in due course he did. However, it was not what I had expected.

Paul told us that he had dinner one evening with an Indian missionary whilst visiting Bangalore. The missionary told Paul that he had been working for some time on a remote island. One day, while he was conducting a Sunday school service with a group of local children, they all heard a massive noise. Upon rushing outside, they saw a wall of water, a tsunami that was clearly going to engulf them. He gathered the children and suggested they play a game which involved running to the highest ground they possibly could. After linking hands, they did just that, just before the entire village was swept away. The buildings were engulfed in water, including the church they had been in. The small group watched in horror as houses were crushed and destroyed. They continued to watch as everything they could identify and every person they knew, including the children's parents, were swept away.

The missionary went on to tell Paul that he was now the guardian of these children. He was still looking for a place where they could live and he could educate them. It was proving to be difficult. He was also trying to raise funds for books and educational materials. Paul looked at him and felt humbled by the way this man was dedicating his life to assist others, with such devotion, and for no material reward. Paul also felt pain at the unfairness of these children not only losing their homes and parents, but also being denied an education and being left to a life of poverty and limited opportunity.

He asked the missionary how much it would cost to initiate a fund to help educate and house the children. The missionary said that it would cost about three and a half thousand dollars to do this. There were twelve children in all. So Paul calculated that roughly the man needed forty-two thousand dollars. Paul asked the missionary "So, three and a half thousand dollars per child. Would that give you somewhere to house them and to educate them?" The missionary replied that it was not three and a half thousand dollars per child but three and a half thousand dollars total. This would give them somewhere to live, eat and be educated. Paul immediately looked at him and said, "It's fixed." He wasn't quite sure how he was going to fix it, but Paul felt for such a small amount of money, these children deserved a real opportunity. He was glad to help and it may have been that both this story and Paul's good work would have ended with this generous act, had it not been for an email Paul received six weeks later.

Using the only computer in the nearest town, the missionary sent Paul a thank-you email with some pictures attached that showed the children being taught and enjoying a meal in their new house. This small one-room house, secured with the funds donated by Paul, would become a catalyst for the rest of their lives. In a closer picture of the front of their house, Paul saw that they had unfurled a banner above the door which read 'Paul Dunn House'. Paul choked back his tears. He was amazed that, for such a relatively small sum of money, he had been able to positively impact a number of lives; it occurred to him that we are here for a reason and we are here for a purpose.

Sometime later, at a mentoring meeting for entrepreneurs in Bali, Paul met a Japanese lady called Masami Sato. Masami had successfully operated a chain of burger joints in Australia and New Zealand which she eventually developed to become a large and profitable supplier of gluten-free frozen products. Masami brought one of her product packages to the Bali meeting and on the side of the carton were the words, 'When you buy this product, you help us to support a soup kitchen in India'. Paul was impressed by both the cleverness of the marketing message and the contribution that the product made. He smiled and made an off-the-cuff remark: "I have heard of buy one get one free, but this is buy one give one." They parted on good terms and Paul went about his business. The following week Masami phoned Paul and mentioned his remark. He was mystified. What remark? "The buy one give one," she replied. "What are you getting at?" asked Paul and Masami said that she had an epiphany on her way back home after meeting Paul and hearing his comment about giving something with each purchase. She had been thinking about the small amount her firm donated to the soup kitchen in India every time they sold one of their products. Surely this idea could work across any market and help better the world? Paul asked her to explain further.

She said, "How would it be, if somebody went to buy a television, that someone else in the world was given the gift of sight? How would it be if when you bought a cup of coffee, a child living in poverty received clean water?"

Paul Dunn immediately saw the opportunity; having been surprised at how little money it had taken to revolutionise the children's lives in India, he had enough of an insight to know that even a small contribution could have a massive impact on the lives of others.

He also realised that giving this way would not be because of guilt or out of obligation. He felt that financing good causes based on peoples' obligation was completely unsustainable. However, a sense of wellbeing would be created if a charity or cause received money every time a purchase was made. Suddenly, consumers would not have to do anything to contribute. Whenever they made a purchase, there would be a feel-good glow that would come from knowing that a small slice of the retail profit would go to improve the life of someone else. As a consumer it would cost no more, and for the vendor of the product, it would cost a tiny amount of overall revenue and the contribution would be massively effective. Not only that, the firm would send a unique message about the way it conducted business. Paul Dunn now had purpose, a massive driver in his life.

Paul and Masami went on to establish Buy1GIVE1. I would urge you to have a look at www.b1g1.com. The Buy1GIVE1 organisation has moved the act of charitable giving from a model driven by ad hoc events to a very specific transaction-based model. It means that we can now all donate in an effortless way when we make purchases. It costs us no more money and takes no more effort. Buy1GIVE1 is a social enterprise that supports people globally and has a massive impact on the lives of millions of people. The Buy1GIVE1 family helps many other charity organisations around the world to create sustainable contribution models. Best of all, Buy1GIVE1 donates 100% of all contributions. The organisation is set up in such a way that all expenses and overheads are paid for by subscribers, meaning that nothing is taken from the contributions it receives and everything goes to good causes. At the last count Buy1GIVE1 was operating in twenty-eight countries and was involved in over six hundred projects. It is a huge purpose-driven enterprise. It fired up Paul Dunn's life and lifted him to new heights.

Purpose as energy:

When you establish purpose in your life, you ignite an energy within you which can impact not only your life, but also on that of your family, friends and colleagues. Purpose has an almost magical power. Clear decisive knowledge of the path you are taking not only drives you, it brings people with you. The quality of self-leadership attracts people to your cause. This is why it is so important to be absolutely clear about your purpose – something which is not easy when we are living busy lives. To spend time examining our values takes time, effort and a degree of self-honesty that few people ever trouble themselves to engage in.

Pinpoint your Purpose:

Personal Best People: Lord Neil Kinnock - former Labour Leader
"Do something that makes a difference."

I once read that thinking is the hardest work there is and this is worth acknowledging. Really understanding our core values, our true beliefs and our real drivers, and questioning what we are doing with our lives is difficult. It stretches us intellectually and emotionally. But your life will change when you determine the answer to these questions. What do you want? What is your purpose? What do you really want to do? True self-leadership comes from understanding this.

Nothing great can happen until you are absolutely clear about what your chief aim is. Be clear about your aim and you will discover your true gift. That clarity allows you to take imaginary scenarios or visions and develop these into a mission, a plan for your life. It allows you to lose yourself in what you love. What do you want? Give yourself the gift right now. Let your imagination run riot. If you knew you would succeed what would you do? Who would you become?

If you have taken the time to ask yourself these questions, you should have started to develop insights that were only vague ideas a short while ago. Change can happen in an instant. The moment of decision is what gives us momentum; making a decision, as we all know, frequently makes us feel good because it puts an end to uncertainty. Most of us have vague ideas about what we would like to achieve but we never take the time clarify our outcomes. So we walk around with these 'someday' ideas. Someday I'll start that business, someday I'll get that qualification, and someday I'll sail around the world. It never happens and life passes us by while we stand and daydream about it.

So, hopefully, you have taken the time for this important bit of self-introspection and you now have an idea of what you want. So why do you want it?

The power of why:

When things get tough, when the road seems uphill, when you encounter challenges, the thing that will keep you going is your Why. The power of your purpose is what will keep you driving forward. The reasons you do what you do, the power behind your ultimate goal is in that word. Why?

Once you know what your outcome is, you need to be clear about why you want it. *What* you want is the desired outcome that acts as the ignition to your dreams. *Why* you want it is the fuel that keeps you moving.

People who succeed and achieve goals are not exceptionally gifted. They are not super beings, they do not possess special mental or physical powers; they just have a bigger reason to make things happen in their lives. They are driven to succeed, whether in business, their career, their relationships or any other area of their life. The difference between them and people who don't succeed is that they have more reasons for wanting or needing to achieve their goals than other people do. Nothing great has been achieved without someone having a big enough why; a reason that drives them through the barriers encountered. If you are going to succeed, you have to know your outcome and the reason you believe it to be important. I am aware of how simplistic this sounds and that you will understand it intellectually. The real challenge, however, is living it. Stretching yourself every day to become your best, pushing yourself to do more, becomes easier if you understand your own motives.

Why you do what you do:

Why do we want anything? Why do we want to start a business? Why do we want to get married? To have kids? To get rich? To get divorced? To go on holiday? To own a BMW? Why?

The reason we do anything is because of how it makes us feel. We are influenced constantly by our feelings. You can test this. Ask anyone what they want and ultimately you will find it is because of how it will make them feel. When people say they want money, they don't particularly want bits of paper with the faces of deceased notables on them. What they want is the freedom that it will give them.

Whatever you want in life is based on how you believe you will feel once you have achieved or acquired it.

Most people answer affirmatively when asked if they would like to be rich. When asked why, they generally respond by saying that wealth provides the freedom to do what they want, whenever they please. They would have the time to do the things they most enjoy and also the ability to help those whom they love. This in turn leads to a more fulfilling and interesting life, and to contentment. And why would they want that? The answer, which would be the same for all of us, is that they want to feel good.

Whatever you want, be it financial freedom, weight loss, a relationship, spiritual connection, or a promotion, it all comes down to how you believe it will make you feel. So if you are setting yourself a primary purpose in life, the real drivers that will propel you towards your goals are the feelings that these achievements will generate for you. Take the time today, and then on a regular basis, to write down your chief purpose and goals close to your heart, to ensure that you are on the right path. Be clear about what you want and why you want it.

If you do nothing else with this book, do answer these two most compelling questions: what do I want and why do I want it? If you are clear about these two factors, you will be further ahead in the quest to realising your aspirations than ninety per cent of your peers.

If these questions seem too big, then ask yourself intelligent leading questions. What do I love to do? What am I good at? What am I passionate about? What do I love to talk about? Usually, you will find both your passion and your purpose within these questions.

Personal Best People: Lynne Sedgmore - Executive Director 157 Group
"I love what I do. For me there is something really important in having "noble work" or "right livelihood". It nourishes the soul and makes life feel good."

Remember you are designing your life, so if your brain comes back with 'I love to sit on the couch and eat ice cream' or 'I am really good at bitching about workmates', you might want to re-evaluate. What would serve your highest purpose? Get clear on this; you'll be glad you did.

The purpose-driven life:

A clear purpose in life is a strong driver to a fulfilled and meaningful existence, but there are other benefits. A strong emotional connection to your purpose can actually help you live longer. In research conducted by the Ruth Alzheimer's Disease Centre in Chicago, a survey was conducted with nearly twelve hundred older adults. The research involved asking each participant about their purpose in life and rating themselves on a score as to how important that purpose was to them and how much it meant to them. When the scores were analysed, the researchers found that the people with a higher sense of purpose had about half the risk of dying during the follow-up period than did those with a lower sense of purpose. This was found to be true even after allowing for external factors such as those who suffered from depression or who had other illnesses or disabilities. The director of this research, Dr Patricia Boyle, said that the results of the analysis indicate that if you find your purpose in life and your life is meaningful, you are likely to live longer. We know this intuitively, and we all hear of people 'losing the will to live', but it is fascinating to find that it is borne out by scientific analysis.

Emerging results from more recent research not only strongly support the evidence that having a purpose in life is critical to maintaining psychological wellness, but also indicates that such a purpose also favourably impacts physical health. In this research Dr Boyle and her colleagues studied retirees who were older than sixty-five, and focused on those who after retiring had done some volunteer work. Again, the results of this study were almost incontrovertible: in a four year follow-up period, the people who volunteered their time and contributed to society had about half the risk of dying compared with those who did not volunteer.

Personal Best People: Craig Sams - Founder Green & Black's Chocolate
"When I was 30 I thought I'd retire at 40. When I was 40, maybe at 50. I'm 67 now and can't imagine retiring."

One of the most startling results came from separate research by American psychologist Dr Mo Wang. He found that people who retired fully were more likely to become unwell, and tended to die earlier than those who continued to work at some level, be it on a voluntary basis, self-employed, or at a temporary job. Dr Wang and his colleagues looked at the United States National Institute statistics on ageing, gained from questioning twelve thousand people about their health, employment history and personal circumstances over a six-year period. Allowing for health issues and other data which could have affected their findings, the research team found that retirees who continued to work in a job experienced less major disease than those who did not. It also found their cognitive reasoning and mental health were better than their peers who had chosen not to continue with some kind of work.

A number of the people I interviewed for this book were well beyond standard retirement age. I met with many in their seventies and eighties, an age when most of their colleagues were long retired or dead. The older achievers I interviewed may not now work as many hours as they did when they were younger (although some did), but it was clear that the notion of not working in some way had not entered their minds. Whatever their background, they seemed to enjoy being busy or at least keeping their hand in. They had an interest on a full or part-time basis and it still formed a central plank of their lives.

Choices:

Right now you do not have to work. You may think you have to work to earn an income, but no one makes you do it, you choose to. The truth is that you have the luxury of choice. You could choose to pitch your tent on some common ground and live off the land. You could choose to go home and explain to your spouse that from now on you will both be living in the car. Or, yes, you can go to work tomorrow and earn an income that allows you to make the payments on your home and cover the household bills. You choose. Most of us do something that earns an income and it is where the majority of our waking hours and effort are expended. We choose to do this because right now, even if we do not like what we do, it allows us to fulfil our caveman needs of shelter and food.

But what a drag to go out and do something you hate, or even something that is just tolerable, in exchange for money. You are spending that most finite of resources, time, doing something that you don't enjoy.

You have three avenues open to you. First you could quit and do something that gives you fulfilment. Secondly, you could re-evaluate your work life to see if it supports you in achieving your life's purpose. Finally, you can suffer on until at some point in the indeterminable future you are pensioned off to live the last few years of your life bitching about all the time you wasted.

Personal Best People: Tony Hsieh – CEO, Zappos
"I would say, rather than focus on what would make you the most money or be best for your career, figure out what you would be passionate about for ten years and go and pursue that. Be true to yourself. If you follow that principle, a lot of decisions are actually pretty easy."

Be clear on this point. You don't *have* to do anything. Just because you qualified as a doctor does not mean you have to continue in the medical profession. The fact that your family enjoys a certain lifestyle because you do what you do is not reason enough either. Being your best means moving away from your comfort level and being ruthlessly honest with yourself about what you want to achieve for yourself and those you love. It could be that you already love what you do, or it could be that your main purpose in life is to give a stable background to your family and your work is simply a means to that end. If so, that is great, but be honest about it. Don't put yourself in the position where twenty years from now you rue the chances missed and agonise about what could have been. The discomfort of asking yourself some fundamental questions right now, about what you want in your life, is nothing compared to the searing pain of regret of an unfulfilled life.

You should be able to tap in to the value of your greatest gifts. Whether you work for an organisation or run your own business, it's important that you are able to develop a clear understanding of where you are going in life and why you are going there.

Many people dream of running their own business, which is great. However, I do meet many seemingly successful business people who are running companies they don't really want to run. They feel trapped into it because this is what makes them an income and others are reliant on them for employment. If you fall into that trap, you can never be fulfilled. It is all too easy to end up doing things both workwise and in our personal lives, solely for financial reward or because of the needs and expectation of others.

American businessman and speaker Jim Rohn talked about life being dangerous. Although a little tongue in cheek, this sentiment is worth understanding. He said, "Life is dangerous. Getting up in the morning is dangerous. Falling in love is dangerous. Crossing the street is dangerous. Having kids is dangerous. It's all dangerous. The fact is life is so dangerous that no one will make it out alive!" The absolute truth is that whatever our religious or spiritual beliefs may be, at some point we will not exist in our current form in this world. All we have is time and none of us knows how much of it we have available to us. So what we do with the time between now and our final moment should be of the highest possible value and should align itself with what we believe is our great purpose in life.

None of us get the opportunity to turn the clock back. But right now you can decide what you want to be and what you want to see in your life. I am not suggesting you throw your intelligence away. If you dreamed of being a premiership footballer and you are now in your seventies, it may be that your chance has gone. But as of today what could you still become? Who do you want to be when you grow up?

Critical questions:

So I hope you took the time to reflect and asked yourself the most critical questions. What do you want? Why do you want it? Whether it takes you one minute or one year, you need to be clear. What is your purpose? What is it you want to achieve? Why do you want to see that achievement in your life? It may be that you need to take it step by step. Maybe other things in your life take precedence. Maybe you don't feel as though you can change direction, quit your job and become an explorer or an astronaut overnight! I know you may have commitments, which means you may take this gradually rather than in one huge leap. But to create an extraordinary life you need to know what your end game is and then take the necessary steps to get there.

So, if you are a postman, you may need to get up tomorrow and deliver post. If you are a salesperson, you have got to go out there and sell. If you are a CEO, you still have to manage and run your company. However, regardless of the minutiae of your life, you still need to know whether you are doing something that is serving your life's purpose. Is it something you want to do for the long term? Get clear on your purpose and the rest of your life will run itself.

I spoke to hundreds of people as part of this project, and all of them were passionate about what they did, because it was their purpose or was in alignment with their purpose. Don't get me wrong. Some of them ran businesses that perhaps they weren't completely smitten by, but it served a bigger goal. It didn't completely satisfy them but it didn't suck the soul out of them either. They had a team that ran their business and the profits their business generated allowed them to do things that were important to them – perhaps running another business or a charitable concern, or pursuing leisure or sporting interests. I'm not saying that every detail and moment of your life has to be spent in exultant bliss, but they all do have to serve your longer term goals in some way. They have to serve your life's purpose.

Here is a great question. What do you want to be famous for? What words would you like people to use when they describe you? Look at the reputation you have today: is it the kind of reputation you want, or would you prefer it enhanced in some way? Let your imagination run wild. Your past is not your future. It doesn't matter where you are coming from.

All that matters is where you are going and if you are clear on your purpose everything else becomes easier.

It's worth taking the time right now to grab a pen and pad to write these questions out longhand and answer them honestly. All you have in this life is time. It is our most precious resource and we can spend it doing almost anything – working, playing, watching TV, goofing around, daydreaming or reading newspapers. So right now I'm asking you if the design of your life is important enough for you to grab a pen and paper and write out these questions and answer them.

What do you want?

Why do you want it?

One of the most humbling experiences I had while writing this book was to speak to someone who had a limited time left to live. The individual still went to work every day and did what he had been doing for the last couple of decades. It occurred to me that this was someone who was fulfilling his purpose. It's not a particularly pleasant thought or one that any of us would like to reflect upon, but if this were the last chapter of your life, the last few months, how would you want to spend it? Would you continue to do the work that you've been doing or would you want to go and do something else completely different?

Your true values surface very quickly. Why wait? Why not decide right now what's important to you and what your purpose is?

Clarity makes your dreams become reality. When you decide what your major definite purpose is in life, it will be a springboard for personal fulfilment and major achievement. Decide upon your major definite purpose. Dare you ask: What do I want? Why do I want it?

CHAPTER 3: **Enthusiasm**

Enthusiasm is the divine particle in our composition: with it we are great, generous, and true; without it, we are little, false, and mean. - Letitia Landon

Our enthusiasm is communicated through our actions, our words, the way we connect with others, how we carry ourselves, how hard we work and our love for life. The origin of the word 'enthusiasm' is the ancient Greek word 'enthousiasmos', which is derived from the adjective 'entheos', meaning 'the god within'. When we have a purpose and are passionate about what we do, we have unbridled energy that carries us through the day. This energy and enthusiasm can seem literal, a messianic like zeal, and can affect us all.

A person may appear to be completely unmotivated and not even have the energy to cross the road, much less have 'a god within'. But if their fire is stoked and they engage in a discussion about a subject they feel strongly about, such as their family or a hobby, we will see a physical change. They become excited and animated as they talk about something they love. If you don't believe me, try criticising a person's religion, political viewpoint or favourite football team. It will be an interesting conversation!

During my meetings with successful people, time after time I noted their almost tangible passion and energy. They were driven and excited about what they did and appeared to go through life at a hundred miles per hour, tackling each obstacle and task with boundless enthusiasm.

Whether the high achievers that I spoke to were discussing their career, business, relationships or family; their energy and zest for life was obvious. Their enthusiasm did not dwindle with age; in fact many retained a hunger to do more. Enthusiasm for life was one of the most common traits that I found amongst all the high achievers I met. For the most part, they simply loved what they did.

Personal Best People: Trevor Baylis - Inventor
"Always always always. I always did something that I loved to do."

So, where does this passion come from? I personally don't think that anybody is born or blessed with it, nor do I feel that any particular people or groups of people are ordained with higher levels of energy, greater mental resources or vitality than others.

I think the fact that high achievers are consistently focusing, driving and working with purpose leads to that energy. When we are enthusiastic, we manage on less sleep, take less days off sick and work more effectively. So what makes the difference? What allows some people to tap into these deep wells of energy, while others appear to sleepwalk through life? We have all heard the adage 'use it or lose it', and this is particularly true of the level of enthusiasm we have for life.

The more energy and vibrancy we give out, the more we seem to have left to give.

Enthusiasm is how Steve Jobs made Apple one of the most innovative and forward thinking companies in the world. It was what made Michelangelo dedicate four years of his life painting the ceiling of the Sistine Chapel and it is what drove Mother Teresa to help the sick and dying.

Children have an unbridled enthusiasm for life, but somewhere along the way it gets lost. There is nothing wrong with going back to that childlike state to ask yourself, 'What do you want to be when you grow up?' What's your goal? What's your dream? How would you spend your time if you were already successful? If money was no object, and time did not matter, what would you do? Sure, we could travel the world and sit on the beach but eventually our life would become meaningless. As we saw in the previous chapter, life without purpose is empty and unsatisfying. Why else would some people who seem to have it all in terms of lifestyle and financial security seem to lead such turbulent lives? Often it seems that when an apparently successful individual has no purpose or inner enthusiasm, they substitute the feeling of excitement with drink, drugs, sex or danger.

Whether we call it enthusiasm, passion or energy, it is a key trait of people who regularly achieve more than others with similar or less resources. How can we get that energy and rediscover our enthusiasm for life?

Well, for a start we can enthuse about whatever we are doing right now, even if we are carrying out a job that we don't particularly like. If we believe that it will lead to bigger, brighter and better tomorrows, that will certainly lead to an increase in our motivation. Almost always, our skill and success in life comes down to our personal motivation.

Personal Best People: Rachel Elnaugh - Entrepreneur
"Positive mindset plus inspired action are the keys to getting results. You really have got to love what you are doing with all your heart. Some people are more interested in making money but that is not the easiest way to success. I have found that many successful people have a similar trait. They have lots of positive energy and that is infectious."

The Job Offer:

If you were offered a job tomorrow and the work involved loading cow manure from early morning until night, how would you feel? Would you be enthusiastic? What if you had to do it for a month? Or that the pay was just one penny per day? Would it be your dream job or not?

Would you feel the excitement of limitless opportunity? How about if it was agreed that you would do this job for thirty days straight, no time off and with just one fifteen-minute break for lunch every day, but that the one penny daily payment would double each day. So that on day one you will receive 1p, on your second day, you will receive 2p, day three a whopping 4p and on the fourth day you would be up to 8p. Are you feeling any better about the situation? If not, grab a calculator and work out how much you would earn over the entire thirty day period. If the pay doubles every day you will find that by day seven you will be paid 64p, day twelve is worth £20.48 and if you can stick at it right up to day twenty you will be paid £5242.88 for that day's work. In fact if you keep going you will discover that the overall payment for a single month of hard, unrelenting, thankless and ultimately pointless work would be a total of £10,737,418.24. Now do you think you could hack this job for a month? Could you jump out of your bed every morning full of enthusiasm when you think of the end game?

Of course, this is a ridiculous scenario, but the point is valid. If we believe that what we are doing will help us to achieve a fantastic goal, we could immediately feel passionate and enthusiastic about it. In the manure shovelling example, we would be motivated to work hard, we would turn up on time, and we would be diligent. Given the pay scale, we would not want to give our employer any reason not to pay us. This doesn't necessarily mean that we love the task at every moment, but we love where it could take us.

Morning people:

Do you know anyone that claims not to be a 'morning person'? I always find it funny when friends of mine say that they find it difficult to get out of bed in the morning. One particular acquaintance says he hates mornings and just the thought of getting up and driving through the cold to get to his office at time when the rest of the world is barely awake has him reaching for the snooze button on his alarm clock. However, on Saturdays he plays golf and does not mind getting up at 5am, preparing a flask of coffee for himself and his golf buddy, getting to the club by 6am and practising for an hour before his 7am tee-off slot. All this before returning home at about 11am, so that he can spend the rest of the day with his young family.

So how can somebody that can barely drag himself to his office before 9am during the week find that he is able to get up at the crack of dawn on Saturday without needing an alarm, drive to the golf course, practise, play his round, drive home and still have the energy to play with his kids? The answer of course is that he has the energetic force of enthusiasm for golf and his family. However, he obviously has less for his work.

My friend is never going to make his living from playing golf; he admits that he isn't a particularly good player. But he has toyed with the idea of setting up a golf tour business in conjunction with a travel agency and I suspect that he would work twice as hard for half of his current salary in order to make a success of his own business. He would also be much happier.

Personal Best People: Mark Turner - CEO OC Group and Director of Ellen MacArthur's World Record Circumnavigation
"I left the navy early much to my father's dismay; I had to pay to get out early and resigned just before the last exam. A friend had started a company making winches for America's Cup sailing teams. I took a gamble and left to join this small company. My father did not speak to me for a long time. For two years, I slept on the floor as we built the business up but I was passionate about it and I wanted to do it. I felt I had to do it."

Every successful person that I spoke to during my research was doing exactly what they wanted to be doing in life. It may be a chicken and an egg situation: are they successful because they are doing something that are passionate about, or did they become passionate about what they ended up doing? It doesn't matter. The fact is that they are enthused about and love what they do. So be enthusiastic, even if you have to tell yourself a white lie and make yourself passionate about what you are doing right now. Get into the habit of being enthusiastic about what you do, about your life, your relationships, and your career. Enthusiasm will open the door to new opportunities and provide a renewed perspective.

ERIC LUBBOCK, LORD AVEBURY

Eric Lubbock was an MP for many years, working tirelessly and with distinction on many human rights causes. When I interviewed him, he was eighty three years old but still maintained his interest in – and active support of – several causes. Eric had been unwell for some years but was open about the situation and even posted scan results onto his blog. He had a rare blood cancer. Eric told me, "The doctors told me I have about three years to live, but only one year of useful activity left." Eric had lived a full and productive life and it would have been perfectly understandable for him to choose to slip quietly into a more private life. But Eric said, "I have no ambition other than to continue with what I am doing." There were no places that he felt compelled to visit, no sights that he wanted to see and nothing that he felt he had to achieve before he died. He simply wanted to keep doing what he had always done and continue to work and speak out for those people whose voices rarely get heard.

Because Eric was already doing what he was most enthusiastic about, he had made a conscious decision to carry on doing exactly what he was already doing as it fulfilled his purpose in life. He was passionate about his work and therefore wouldn't choose to do anything else.

Stop working, start living:

Work isn't work if you do what you love. If you get up every day and do something that is in complete alignment with your values, it does not feel like work and creates the freedom to enable you to gain your own personal fulfilment.

Personal Best People: Brad Feld - CEO The Foundry Group
"I fell in love with creating things with a computer. When I was 17, I spent the summer as the first employee for a start-up. I wrote several products for them, got paid $10 per hour, but also got 5% of gross revenue. When I was a freshman in college I'd regularly get checks for $2500 or $5000 for royalties. I realized early in my adulthood that I could spend my time creating what I wanted to create, get paid for it, and explore fascinating new things."

You have to ask yourself whether you are truly enthused about what you do. If you do what you do out of an obligation to others, or solely because it provides you with money, or because of the expectations of others, you need to realise that sooner or later it will cause you some distress.

We have all heard the saying, 'If you do what you love, you will never work a day in your life', and this seemed to be particularly true of the people I spoke to while researching this book. If you are not already doing what you want to do for the rest of your life, clarify what it is that you want and work towards it. If you are working towards anything other than fulfilling your passion, your time is being wasted.

THE 74-YEAR-OLD BOY WONDER

At an age when most men have long since retired, Trevor Baylis still bubbles with enthusiasm for his work and his life. Talking to Trevor is like talking to a five-year-old on Christmas Eve and the world feels like a more exciting place. Trevor is an incredible person whose sheer love for life makes other people feel better just by speaking to him.

Trevor was born before the Second World War; in his youth he was an enthusiastic swimmer and won national honours in the sport. When he talks of his life and his career, he is talking about love. Trevor has always done something that he loved, something he enjoyed and that filled him with enthusiasm. Even when speaking to him today, his passion is clear because the things that fill his life immerse and interest him.

Trevor's father was an engineer, his mother a thespian and both seem to have had an influence on their son's colourful career choices. Although best known as an innovative British inventor, it is less well-known that Trevor also worked as a stuntman after his National Service and used the money he earned from underwater escapes to set up a swimming pool company. The pools were particularly popular as they were the first free-standing type to be available in the UK and their simple installation encouraged schools all over the country to buy them.

Trevor's inventiveness came to the fore, when, after seeing a number of his stunt friends suffer serious injuries which sometimes caused permanent disabilities, he decided to create products to help to make their everyday activities a little easier to perform. Trevor needed to understand the issues that affect people who don't have full use of their physicality, but rather than attempt to gain this knowledge intellectually, he secured one of his arms to his side with a belt and spent days on end with only one functioning arm in order to fully understand the challenges. This exercise enabled Trevor to fully appreciate the difficulties that people with physical disabilities have with everyday tasks, and he was then able to go on to invent several devices to help them.

When AIDS was recognised as being a world-wide problem in the late 1980s, Trevor was watching a TV programme about the spread of the disease. Trevor told me, "I could have been watching Strictly Come Dancing or anything else, but I just happened to be watching a programme about the spread of Aids throughout Africa. They said the only way they could stop the disease was by spreading information and the best way to do this was by the use of radio. But the problem was most of Africa did not have electricity and batteries were expensive."

Using his knowledge of electric motors and the various ways in which they could be powered, Trevor took an electric motor from a toy car and the clockwork mechanism from a music box, and created a rough prototype of the first wind-up radio. Although he patented his idea, it was universally rejected by prospective manufacturers when he tried to get the prototype into production. Despite this, he battled on and told me, "I would work eighteen-hour stretches at a time, fall asleep in my clothes, then wake up and start work again. Although I was exhausted, the work had become pure pleasure."

Trevor continued to try to get his radio into production and recalls being portrayed in the media as a nutty professor, especially following rejections from the design council and being turned down by potential parts suppliers, who had told him that his idea was unworkable. Trevor persisted with his idea for five years and remained convinced that it could positively impact the lives of millions of people. Eventually, after featuring on the BBC science programme

Tomorrow's World, Trevor received some investment and formed the Freeplay Energy Company.

Trevor saw his product become a reality in 1995 when the first Freeplay radios came off an assembly line in Cape Town. As he watched his design become a reality, he remembered the many battles and rejections he had experienced in order for it to be possible. Tears welled in his eyes as he looked around the newly built manufacturing facility and the largely disabled workforce who were producing his award-winning clockwork radio. Immediately after the visit, Trevor met with Nelson Mandela, and the South African President congratulated him on his achievement.

The Freeplay radio went on to be widely distributed throughout Africa and was used as a vital communication and educational tool. It enabled people who had no other means of listening to the news to access several media channels, and allowed information to be distributed amongst communities that had previously been cut off.

None of this would have happened without the English inventor's unbridled enthusiasm and his belief and passion in what he did. Trevor continues to invent today and has numerous patents to his name. He is most proud of Baylis Brands which helps inventors to get their creations to market. Trevor says it best: "I can only say to people that you have to love what you do."

Love what you do:

The love for what they did was a theme reiterated by virtually everyone that I interviewed during my research for this book. A fundamental characteristic of successful people is their passion and purpose in their own life. If you want to become your best, you need to get into that mindset. What are you passionate about? What do you love? Write it down and keep on writing. Don't think about it as you write, don't do it from a mature perspective or second-guess what you will write. What are you truly passionate about?

Personal Best People: Sir Tom Farmer - Founder Kwik-Fit Group
"If you want to succeed in business, you have got to have enthusiasm, you have got to have energy and it has got to be an obsession and it has to be a magnificent obsession."

Regardless of personal issues or perceived financial constraints, we all need to do what we really want to do and when we do what we love, the success, including financial rewards, of our venture will follow. This requires us to have total faith in ourselves and our vision. Most people are afraid of perceived risks and potential failure – but what is there to be afraid of? We should be more afraid of living half a life, a life that doesn't allow us to keep the promises that we made to ourselves or that doesn't allow us to become the person we believe we can be.

Maybe you want more freedom to be with your family, or perhaps you want to start your own business, or change your profession or do something completely different with your life. All of us have heard that persistent voice in our minds, telling us to grab an opportunity or to follow our hearts. The inner voice that tells us to go for it is our inner enthusiasm and intelligence; it is our true self.

If we are in a job, relationship or situation that doesn't make us happy, we need to re-evaluate or change it. Even if it makes us uncomfortable, just because the job is what pays the bills or because we feel various personal obligations, this is not a good enough reason. Listen to your inner voice. Listen, because no matter how hard you try to suppress that voice and the accompanying feelings, you know intuitively that you should follow the message because it aligns with what you love, and needs to be listened to. Change can be instantaneous and only requires that we admit to ourselves what we really want to do with our life. We can change and become contagiously enthusiastic.

The sad truth is, however, that we let fear and doubt separate us from the things we love to do. We do not always appreciate the abundant opportunities that we have been afforded; we don't always appreciate that we don't have to do anything that we don't want to do. We have choices: whether to work or not to work; whether to work or play, whether to be in a relationship or not, whether to continue down one path or move to another one. We are blessed to live in a democratic society that affords us all of those choices. Yet we often take the view that we are restricted and cannot change anything. Nothing could be further from the truth; we have the opportunity and choice to follow our passion.

THE BLOSSOMEST BLOSSOM

Dennis Skinner is one of the longest-serving Members of Parliament. His direct approach and acid tongue have earned him the nickname 'The Beast of Bolsover'. A staunch Socialist and true conviction politician, he has never served on All-Party Parliamentary Group despite his experience, nor does he eat with his parliamentary colleagues in the Commons dining room. He refuses to take trips, even on parliamentary business overseas when he feels that they are paid for by the taxpayer, and against tradition, he always remains in the House of Commons throughout the Queen's Speech and State Opening of Parliament.

Dennis was elected MP for Bolsover in 1970 and has held the seat ever since – although he has been suspended from the House on ten occasions, often for using unparliamentarily language. It is fair to say that Dennis is not a man to be trifled with but when I suggested a meeting, he guardedly agreed.

Despite his fearsome reputation, Dennis's enthusiasm is still as evident as ever when it comes to communicating his ideals. However, he now has the additional energy of a man granted a second chance.

Dennis told me that some years ago and only a short time after undergoing a lifesaving heart bypass operation, he had been diagnosed with cancer. Dennis had always said that he would retire at the next general election but now he feared the worst and it seemed that circumstances would overtake him. But following intensive treatment, Dennis was given the all clear and recalls seeing the world in a different light as he walked from the Chelsea Royal Hospital back to Westminster. He told me, "On the way back from the hospital I looked at a blossom tree. I am sure I had passed it before and never really noticed it. But I now looked at this tree and saw how beautiful it was. I thought it had the blossomest blossom I had ever seen." Life was his again and opportunity once more lay in front of him.

Seize the moment:

Why wait? Why should we wait until a seismic event or news changes our perceptions of life? Being grateful for where we are right now and for the opportunities that lie in front of us are the greatest starting points. Do you remember your mother telling you to count your blessings? She was absolutely right. Developing a grateful attitude and feeling thankful for all the experiences and skills you have provides you with a great platform on which to build a whole world of new opportunities. Be grateful about what you have, be excited by the possibilities, and free the enthusiasm and energy that is contained within you.

Do you have emotions that you do not always share? Do you have dreams that even those people who are closest to you don't know about? What are you waiting for? Admit to yourself what it is that you want and follow it through; this will have a massive, positive impact on your life. Listen to your inner voice.

How one voice can make a change

During the 2008 US Presidential campaign, Barack Obama fell behind Hillary Clinton, his main rival for the Democratic nomination. Clinton's campaign had gathered momentum; it had the support of the party's establishment and was better funded. It began to look as though Barack Obama's attempt to become the first black American President was set to fail and like many nominees before him, it seemed increasingly likely that he would not win his party's ticket, much less have the opportunity to take a run at being President.

During a campaign meeting Obama asked Anne Parks, a legislator in South Carolina, whether he could expect her nomination in the upcoming caucus election.   Parks replied that if Obama committed to come to her hometown and conduct a rally in Greenwood, she would probably vote for him. What Parks did not mention, however, was that Greenwood was distant from the main infrastructure within the state.

By the time the visit came around, Obama's campaign had lost even more momentum and he was somewhat dispirited. After a long day, he trudged into his hotel sometime after midnight, and was planning to go home to see his wife and children the next day. It had been some time since he had seen them and he was looking forward to spending a few days at home. However, his assistant reminded him of his commitment to go to Greenwood the following morning and that he would have to leave at 6 a.m. Obama went to bed in a terrible state and when he woke the next morning, he felt even worse. He tells the story of how he wandered to the window and looked outside to see that it was a grey, miserable day and rain was falling hard. His mood worsened even further when he looked at the New York Times to find an article had been written which indicated that his campaign was about to come off the rails entirely. After coffee, as he walked out to his car, his umbrella blew open and he got soaked. He was now tired, wet and by his own admission, very grumpy.

When Obama arrived at the rally in Greenwood he walked into the room to find that only twenty people had come out to meet him. These people looked tired, overworked and sick of the weather but nonetheless, Obama went straight into campaign mode shook hands, talked to people and asked questions. He began to speak about his hopes and his vision for the future of America but his flow was interrupted when a voice from behind him shouted out, "Fired up!" He turned around but could not identify who had spoken. He began speaking again. The voice repeated, "Fired up!" This time the audience jokingly joined in and replied, "Fired up!" He turned around and this time the voice said, "Ready to go! Fired up! Ready to go!"

Barack Obama now saw who had interrupted his speech, a middle-aged supporter called Edith Childs. The candidate kept his gaze on Edith but she stared back at him and yelled again "Fired up! Ready to go!" The audience, warming to the theme, shouted back, "Fired up! Ready to go!" Every time Childs yelled, "Fired up! Ready to go!" the audience replied in kind. Obama said later that as these incantations were flying around the room, he stood at the podium, trying to figure out what exactly was going on. He couldn't fathom it but he liked the sentiment. Eventually, he started shouting, "Fired up! Ready to go!" The chant then took fire and effectively became one of Obama's key campaign slogans along with 'Yes we can'. His point of retelling the story was that one voice can change a room just as it did that day. Obama went on to win ten straight election victories which got him the Democratic nomination and ultimately the Presidency.

The President said that if one voice can change a room, it can change a city. If it can change a city, it can change a state. If it can change a state, it can change a nation. And if it can change a nation, it can change the world. On that day, Edith Childs' voice did indeed, change the world.

Change the world:

Approaching life with enthusiasm, with fire in your belly, with a never-say-die attitude, can change your life and indeed the world. It comes down to deciding what you are passionate about. Because whatever drives your enthusiasm isn't just what you should be doing with your life, it is what you must be doing with your life.

CHAPTER 4: **Resilience**

All the adversity I've had in my life, all my troubles and obstacles have strengthened me. You may not realize it when it happens, but a kick in the teeth may be the best thing in the world for you. - Walt Disney

In all the interviews that I conducted during my research, not one person spoke of their life in terms of an ever-upward trajectory of unbridled success. Nobody reflected on a life that had been unencumbered by obstacles or difficulties. Whatever field you go into, you will meet some form of resistance and part of your journey has to be to learn how to overcome it. Resilience is the determination to keep going when things do not go to plan, and the strength to push through obstacles or find a way around barriers. As Tony Robbins, the American business and life coach says, "If you can't find a way, you must make a way."

Personal Best People: Lord David Alton - Author and Human Rights Campaigner
"Sometimes the best learning is done at the University of Adversity."

The inner confidence of people who are successful in their chosen field often seems to imply that they have gone through life bouncing from one achievement to the next. But everyone I spoke to had encountered challenges, usually several, and some had also met with tragedy and seemingly impossible circumstances. All of them had suffered fears or doubts at some point, mainly about running out of money or suffering the embarrassment of failure. What made the difference was that they developed an inner steel, the determination and discipline to see things through.

Overnight success is rare. When we read of somebody who sells a company for a hundred million dollars, having launched it only a few years earlier, it is news, but the reason that it is newsworthy is because it rarely happens. Even in instances of people who seem to come from nowhere to prominence in a short space of time, there is usually a backstory. We tend to find that behind this seemingly effortless success, there are many years of hard work, failure, restarting and re-educating themselves, learning how not to do something before they finally break through. We only see the successful part of their journey; the hours spent alone and all the sleepless nights are lost to us. We all feel inspired when we hear of someone achieving a massive breakthrough. The truth is usually less glamorous and is usually testament to the fact that great success cannot be achieved without great resilience.

Kids and candy:

In 1972, Walter Michelle at Stanford University carried out a fascinating experiment known as 'The Marshmallow Experiment'. The study involved offering a child a marshmallow. Each participant was offered the choice between eating one marshmallow immediately or two marshmallows after the researcher had returned back into the room from 'an errand', during which time the single marshmallow was left in front of the children.

The children were observed remotely while the researcher was out of the room. Those who had decided to wait for the two marshmallows could usually wait for a moment or two and would then begin to fidget; some averted their eyes so they were unable to see the marshmallow that they had been offered and others turned around so they could not see the tray. In desperate attempts to distract themselves from the sweet the children would tug on pigtails, kick their chair or they would stroke the marshmallow as if they were stroking a favourite pet.

Of the six hundred children who took part in the experiment, only a minority chose to eat a marshmallow immediately. Of those who chose the second option, one-third managed to wait long enough to win themselves a second marshmallow; the other children surrendered to temptation before the researcher returned.

A follow-up study many years later showed that the pre-school children who had delayed gratification for longer had gone on to achieve higher scores in their exam results, indicating that the characteristics and self-discipline revealed in childhood remained with these people for their whole lives.

What is resilience?

Resilience can be broken down into two component parts, determination and discipline. The lack of either of these qualities prevents more dreams from becoming reality than virtually anything else. Many people start off with exciting plans of what they want to achieve, but stop as soon as they hit an obstacle. They give up because it seems too hard, but worthwhile achievements are rarely handed to us. If we decide that life is not fair and that we can't achieve our desired outcomes due to some external factor, we are just surrendering our dreams. The real danger is that if we give up on something once, it will become easier to give it up second time round. Before long we have developed a habit of giving up and before much longer we abandon all our hopes and aspirations. However, if we are living a purpose-driven life, if we are passionate about our outcomes, we will have the resilience to achieve our goal, no matter what happens.

Personal Best People: Robert Edmiston - Chairman IM Group
"Perseverance, clarity of thought and providence are the major
characteristics that have helped me. Stay focused. Plan for the worst, hope
for the best. So long that you have the downside covered, you don't have to
keep looking over your shoulder."

Determination determines your future:

Throughout history there are examples of determination delivering people to their destinies. Abraham Lincoln suffered eight election defeats, two failed businesses, the death of his fiancée and a nervous breakdown before he became one of the most highly regarded US Presidents. Henry Ford is credited with bringing the motor car to the masses, but he wasn't an instant success. When he initially tried to launch himself as a car manufacturer, he failed and was left penniless; it was only over a period of time that he achieved success and created the Ford Motor Company that we know today. Media star Oprah Winfrey suffered a traumatic and abusive childhood and in her early teens gave birth to a child which died only weeks after being born. Oprah reflected on this moment in her life and said at the time she was emotionally detached from the situation, such was the pain that she had suffered and inadequacy she felt. But despite this tumultuous start to her life, she went on to become one of the warmest, empathetic and recognised personalities in the world.

GLENN CUNNINGHAM

At the beginning of the last century, eight-year-old Glenn Cunningham attended school in a small cabin that served as the local schoolhouse in Elkhart, Kansas, where he lived. The room in which he and his classmates were taught was heated by a coal stove; Glenn and his older brother Floyd went to school early each day to start the fire so that the room was warm by the time their teacher and classmates arrived. The fire was usually started with kerosene, but when the boys arrived one day, the container had mistakenly been filled with gasoline and the fire roared out of control before either boy could react. The teacher arrived to find the schoolhouse in flames and realising the boys were inside, he rushed at the door and managed to pull Glenn free. However, Floyd tragically died in the fire. The doctor who treated Glenn told his mother that it was likely that Glenn would also die and the only consolation the doctor could offer was that, given the severity of his injuries, it would probably be for the best. The fire had removed virtually all the skin from Glen's legs and the lower half of his body.

To the physician's surprise Glenn did not die. His determination and will to live humbled the hospital staff. They provided the boy with the best care available and slowly he began to respond to treatment. Despite this, the doctors recommended that Glenn's legs be amputated because of his crippling injuries. They could not be repaired and there was a risk that they could become infected, causing additional complications in what was already a tremendously difficult recovery.

His mother declined to take the advice and Glenn was discharged from hospital. Although he still had his legs, they were useless and lifeless. When Glenn got home he pledged that he would walk again.

One morning while sitting in the family garden, Glenn slid from his wheelchair onto the grass and dragged himself over to the fence which separated his home from the road. Using a wooden post, he gradually pulled himself up and balanced himself into a semi-upright position. He then hand-walked along the length of the fence, dragging his lifeless legs behind him. This became a daily routine and Glenn's mother allowed it, although in her mind it was only in order to give her boy some hope. Over a period of time Glenn's trailing legs wore a smooth path on the lawn but eventually, through sheer force of will and helped by physical therapy, Glenn managed to stand unaided. It was nearly two years later that he began to take his first, faltering steps but soon after that he was able to walk and just a few months later, remarkably, he was able to run.

Glenn returned to school and having been denied the use of his legs for so long he started to run there. He also ran when he was sent on errands. He ran simply for the joy of being able to run. Later, in college, Glenn became such a proficient runner that he made the track team, and his speed over almost any distance earned him the nickname 'The Elkhart Express'.

Glenn Cunningham was a quietly spoken young man, who had seemed unlikely to live through the trauma of his injuries. But he went on to become one of the United States' most successful middle distance runners. He set world records in 800 metre and mile events as well as winning a silver medal at the 1936 Berlin Olympics. Today in Elkhart you can walk (or run) through Cunningham Park, named after the town's most famous son.

Determination is one of the ways in which we can recognise our inner strength. It is the courage we generate, the resoluteness of purpose that we feel, it is the setting of standards that we refuse to fall short of. Determination carries us forward against overwhelming odds and allows us to stay focused and certain of our desired outcome. Determination is the cornerstone of developing irresistible resilience.

Discipline... keep on keeping on:

Personal Best People: Carl Elsener Jr- CEO Victorinox, makers of the Swiss Army Knife
"Perseverance, patience, the courage to make decisions and creativity have stayed with me throughout my personal and professional life. I was always good at sticking with things even if I did not succeed at the first attempt."

The second key element of resilience is discipline, the ability to do what many other people don't – turning up early and working diligently and quietly until the job is complete.

Self-discipline is being able to take action despite external factors or distractions and regardless of your current emotional state. During my interviews the thread of self-discipline ran through every story. People who achieve their goals are not always the most talented or the most qualified; they are not always the most skilled in their field. But they are able to rise above the crowd because they do what has to be done. Their discipline means that they are able to complete the tasks they need to, day after day, in order to achieve their goals. Self-discipline can be developed, just like building muscle. The more we train our body, the stronger it becomes. The more we ask of ourselves and the more we push ourselves each day, the more capacity and self-discipline we develop. Albert Einstein said of himself, "It's not that I'm so smart, I just stay with the problem longer."

No matter what goals we have, we will experience some resistance before we achieve them and will have to rethink, retry and recalibrate some elements of our journey.

Think of a modern torpedo that has inbuilt intelligence systems which allow changes in direction while heading towards a moving target. The torpedo's 'brain' will assess the feedback provided by the guidance system and change direction accordingly. The torpedo does not get upset or give up and head back to the mother ship. It simply adjusts course while continuing to move forward. So whenever you have any upsets or disappointments you should accept it as feedback, make any necessary adjustments – but keep moving forward. Tireless resilience will prevail.

JOANNE

Joanne is unable to remember when her depression started but she became aware of it in her late teens. She feels that despite her constant efforts to win her father's approval, she never succeeded. Her mother, who Joanne was much closer to, was diagnosed with multiple sclerosis when Joanne was only fifteen. Although her mother struggled with the disease for the next ten years, she eventually lost the battle and when she died Joanne felt completely alone in the world as she had lost contact with her father entirely by this time.

Subsequently, Joanne met and married a man and moved to his home in Portugal where she taught English. She felt as happy as she could ever remember being and soon became pregnant with a daughter who she called Jessica. Sadly, Joanne and her husband separated after a few months and Joanne moved to Scotland to be near to her sister who lived in Edinburgh.

Despite the close proximity of a family member, Joanne entered a spiral of fear and doubt and was diagnosed with clinical depression. She confesses to having contemplated suicide but attempted to rebuild her life again by taking a teaching course and moving into a small flat with Jessica. Joanne had no earned income and relied on welfare state payments while she attended teaching college. It was now nearly seven years since she had graduated from university and she felt like a failure; her marriage had failed almost before it started; she was jobless and had a dependent child.

At rock bottom, Joanne started to write again, just as she had done in her childhood. She reflected upon her life and wrote about many subjects, even going back to an idea involving a children's book that had come to her many years earlier. Joanne found that writing was a great release. It allowed her to live through the characters in her book, a welcome escape from the harsh realities of her life.

Joanne discovered that taking Jessica out for a walk was the only way to get the child to sleep and thus give her some time to quietly write. So she got into a routine of taking the toddler out in her pushchair and when she nodded off, Joanne would take Jessica into a warm cafe. As the child slept, Joanne, cradling a single cup of coffee, would write.

Over the next two years, Joanne finished her book and sent the manuscript to a number of publishers but only received muted responses and out-of-hand rejections in return. A full year later, a small publishing house in London wrote to Joanne and offered her an advance of fifteen hundred pounds. Joanne couldn't have been happier. Although the advance was modest, it was a small fortune to her and even better, her book would be on the shelves in bookshops.

The publisher warned her that there was very little chance that she would make any money and that she should not expect to live off the income generated by the book. She decided that writing was a vocational task: very few children's authors ever make enough money to live entirely on their earnings from writing. Joanne didn't care. She had proved something to herself and now knew that she could write a book that would be shared with the world, in a small way perhaps, but it was enough.

The publisher decided to print one thousand copies. To Joanne's surprise and that of her publisher, the book won a prize in children's literature and became more well-known as a result. A year later, an auction was held in the United States for the rights to publish the book outside Europe. To her amazement, the bidding went to $105,000. Joanne says that she was shocked when she heard the news; she would now be able to write full-time. She was so excited, she got to work immediately.

Millions of people all over the world are glad that Joanne had the fortitude and resilience to write that book and the others that followed. The books are published under the pen name J. K. Rowling, the name famous worldwide for bringing Harry Potter to life and creating some of the fastest-selling books in history. The movie franchise has broken all box office records and Joanne is regarded as the most successful writer of her generation.

Resilience and adversity:

Personal Best People: Martin Dunphy - CEO Marlin Capital
"How you react to adversity is more important than the event itself."

How we deal with adversity comes down to something that we have already looked at and will continue to look at throughout this book. Our resilience is governed by the intelligent questions that we ask. And the quality of the questions that we ask ourselves reflects the quality of our lives. So when something goes wrong, there is no point in shaking our fist at the sky and becoming angry or asking, 'Why did this have to happen to me?' We have to ask ourselves an empowering question – What can we learn from this? What is good about this? How can we make things better? Asking in this way is resilience in action and provides us with the tools to see our task through.

Resilience and inner strength:

We are often tested on the road to achieving our goals. Sometimes the challenges are small inconveniences and sometimes they are life-altering tests such as serious illness, an accident, the loss of employment or the death of a loved one. These challenges provide an opportunity to appreciate the ups and downs of life a little more than otherwise we might have done. It is a sad fact that it is only when we lose something that we truly understand the value of it.

When the initial shock of a disaster wears off, people tend to develop a sense of thankfulness and a gratitude for the opportunities that they have. In turn a new opportunity is offered to develop different personal philosophies and stronger beliefs about what is important to them. It may kick start them into taking action, or motivate them to grasp opportunities. But why wait until disaster strikes? The time to grasp goals and opportunities is now – but be aware that there will probably be a few bumps on the road ahead. However, if these challenges are accepted as feedback and we have the resilience shown by high achievers, we will come out the other side stronger and wiser.

We will develop an inner strength; a strength that cannot be bought or faked, and one that comes from having faced the most difficult points in our life and overcome them.

ADAM PATEL

As a young man Adam Patel came to England from India. He had three pounds and fifty pence in his pocket, because that is all the Indian government would allow people emigrating to take out of the country. Adam's life was a challenge; he told me, "I worked in a wool mill between 6.00 a.m. to 6.00 p.m. and I would then go on to study accountancy in the evening. I did this for six years with no financial or family support and no one else to come home to." The years of study and discipline eventually paid off and Adam qualified as an accountant. After considering his options Adam decided that rather than working as a clerk in an accountancy office, he would be better served by starting his own business. The fabric trade was flourishing in North East England at the time and Adam's work ethic served him well in the industry. His determination to succeed motivated him to work long hours, without a day off or holiday for several years.

Within a few years his business was booming. It was around this time that the young entrepreneur was speaking to his uncle, who had observed his nephew's achievement and now offered him some advice. He suggested that Adam, who had shown such disciplined fortitude since he had arrived from India, should look at the current opportunities available in Africa. The resource-rich continent was throwing off the shackles of colonialism, revealing great promise and opportunity. Adam assessed the situation and discovered that a multitude of emerging opportunities were indeed available. He had the courage to become an immigrant once more and left England to set up a new business in Zambia. But despite hard work and Adam's best efforts, his business was taken from him a few months later, when a civil war erupted in the country. Adam lost all the money he had earned in the previous years and was unable to get back home. He worked for the Zambian Government just to make ends meet and it was eighteen months before he eventually returned to England. He approached his previous suppliers and explained the situation. Fortunately his reputation was solid, and he was able to obtain a little credit to assist him in restarting a cash and carry business.

Adam said, "I got back to work, I worked sixteen hours a day, seven days a week." Over the next twenty years, Adam turned his business into a multi-million pound company; he also found time to help local voluntary organisations and became a valued community leader. Adam became Lord Patel of Blackburn in 2000. Newspaper reports on his arrival in the House of Lords said merely that Lancashire-based businessman Adam Patel had been made a Lord and would sit on the Labour benches. This is the story that people see. At first glance, it appears that a millionaire businessman, who has led a gilded life, has been given even more influence and privilege. The stories do not tell us about the thirty plus years of striving, difficulty and obstacles that Adam had to overcome. They do not tell us that Adam, without a support structure or financial backing, and at the third time of asking, built a business that is still thriving and that his work within the local community helps other people in many ways.

Adversity is not something most of us welcome into our lives, but overcoming problems strengthens our ability to overcome other challenges. Is suffering necessary for growth? Maybe and maybe not, but it is worth noting that great things have been achieved when people have been in their darkest places. When real challenges are faced, people are able to dig deep within themselves and draw from a well of resources that they wouldn't otherwise have known that they had.

Personal Best People: Sir Chris Evans - Biotech' Entrepreneur
"My advice is to never ever give up and back yourself to win."

THE GARDENER'S STORY

One day a gardener working on his flower beds found the cocoon of a butterfly. When he looked more closely he could see a small opening appear in the cocoon and decided to sit for a few moments to watch the caterpillar emerge and become a butterfly. However, the process took longer than he had anticipated and he went back to his work.

When he returned several hours later he noticed that virtually no progress had been made. He watched and waited again. The butterfly was trying to squeeze out of a tiny hole in the top of the cocoon. The gardener could see it try for a minute at a time before, seemingly exhausted, it sank back to rest. In pity, the gardener reached into his toolbox, pulled out a small pair of scissors, and as gently as possible snipped around the hole and down the side of the cocoon. This freed the butterfly, which then emerged easily into the sunlight. The gardener expected it to open its wings and fly away, but it didn't and only then did he notice its swollen body and small shrivelled wings.

The butterfly never did fly away and spent the rest of its life crawling around that flower bed. What the gardener hadn't understood was that the tiny hole which was keeping the butterfly within the cocoon was nature's way of forcing fluid from its body into its wings, so that it would be ready for flight when it emerged from the cocoon.

The lesson is that sometimes struggles are necessary. If we were to go through life without obstacles, it may cripple us, we would not be as strong as we could have been and we may never fly.

CHAPTER 5: **Specialise**

One reason so few of us achieve what we truly want is that we never direct our focus; we never concentrate our power. Most people dabble their way through life, never deciding to master anything in particular. - Anthony Robbins

In 2011, the UK suffered one of the most turbulent economic years in its history. The effects of recession and shrinking credit markets dramatically affected all sectors. Unemployment was rising, the service sector was shrinking, and consequently one of the toughest businesses to be involved in at this time was recruitment. Finding and supplying people at a time when more people were losing their jobs than were getting hired was difficult. However, a number of recruitment companies broke the trend.

Recruiter magazine, an industry trade publication, lists the top 50 fastest-growing recruitment businesses. The majority of companies on this list all specialise in a specific market; they focus on one area of recruitment rather than simply offering a general service to companies in all sectors. They provide services to niche vertical markets, such as healthcare, financial services, information technology or the oil industry. They concentrate solely on providing an end-to-end recruitment solution for companies within the selected industry. Very few companies who offer multi-sector or general recruitment services appear on the Recruiter magazine list. This trend is not only true in recruitment. In every sector of business now, value is placed on expertise; consumers and companies are attracted to niche specialists. They have more trust in those who can demonstrate experience and knowledge within their sector.

Respond to change:

The world is changing and we all have to be able to respond to that change. Since the middle of the last century, right up to the current day, the Western world has seen a shift in many business and manufacturing processes. Heavy industry has left these shores, perhaps forever. If workers in other parts of the world can punch rivets into the side of a ship for a wage nearly seventy per cent lower than that paid to a European or North American worker, it becomes an economic inevitability that most manufacturing will be carried out overseas.

This isn't only true in heavy industry. Increasingly, expertise from developing countries means that I.T. and customer services jobs are also moving to other parts of the globe. As technology develops in emerging countries and education becomes more widely available, the number of people with skills and expertise will increase, resulting in our economy sustaining further losses of key roles and jobs. As well as affecting today's economy, the increasing skills and levels of knowledge in other parts of the world will also impact our children and their children. No jobs will be safe from other nations which are able to integrate ability and technology in order to produce the same or even better work at a lower cost.

Personal Best People: Craig Sams - Founder Green & Blacks Chocolate
"Somebody somewhere can do almost anything better and more cheaply than you can. If you can get somebody else to do the work you aren't good at or don't like, it gives you more time to do the work you do like. You have more time to make strategic decisions and indulge your imagination if you're not dealing with the minutiae of managing stuff you don't really need to do."

In order to protect yourself from this seismic change, you will need to specialise. All the successful people that I interviewed had developed a deep knowledge in what they do; they have become experts in their chosen field. By constantly stretching yourself to develop new insights and innovations, you can become a leader in whatever area you choose. In order to grow and succeed you will need to develop a specialised knowledge. Moreover, rather than waiting to sit an industry related exam or professional periodic test, choose to increase your knowledge and understanding of your work constantly and consistently.

The theory of expertise:

One of the reasons I spent so much time interviewing successful people is that I wanted to increase my own knowledge regarding what works and what does not. I am constantly seeking to increase my understanding of the theory of expertise. It is all very well to have a theory, even a well-tested theory, but in order to expand my knowledge and understanding I spent two years taking time out to interview and study people who had achieved personal success. By doing so, I developed both my own knowledge as well as an ability to communicate the key areas in which we can all improve. It didn't just reveal the primary traits of successful people to me, but also gave me a powerful insight as to how we can all duplicate the success that they achieve.

The BEST formula that we will look at in the second half of this book relates to understanding how winners win, how some people achieve massive results. The question to ask yourself is: what is the gap between where you are now and your becoming an expert in your field? What knowledge do you need to acquire? Where can you get it? What insights do you need to gain? Another great way of asking this is: what do your customers want? What value could you give them? What understandings of the market or their particular industry can you provide that would create real value for them?

Adding value:

Personal Best People: David Meerman Scott - Marketing Expert and
Bestselling Business Author
"The key difference in getting to the top is that you need to bring something
new. I think that's true of any business."

Your rewards in life will be driven by the amount of value you create for others. That is why it is so important to develop key knowledge; you need it to serve your customers or clients and consequently yourself.

If you focus on becoming an expert or specialist in what you do, the value that you offer others and the value that you command for yourself grows. Whatever their discipline everybody wants a broad range of knowledge, but by focusing on the most valuable elements and developing niche skills within your area of expertise, you will develop huge worth. People are sometimes concerned that if they only concentrate on certain areas, they may become too narrow-minded, too polarised and unable to adapt to changes in circumstance. But there is a difference between specialising and being completely self-absorbed in one area. By focusing on the things that provide value, you will become stronger and more robust. You will be more open to discovering new areas within your field. The confidence that comes with being an expert will be immediately visible to those around you.

You will have an intimate understanding of what is important, and this value will be communicated in everything that you do.

Focus:

This understanding and focus on a specific area was a common theme with most of the people that I interviewed. They each had a laser beam focus on their subject matter. Whether they started a business, were involved in the arts, sports, sciences or followed a particular political or religious path, they all displayed an unwavering focus on what they did. The adage 'stick to your knitting' might sound boring, but it works. If you are in business, you might be tempted by the path of archetypal entrepreneurs; starting new ventures and opening new markets. There are some people who do this successfully. Richard Branson is a prime example of someone who has diversified his interests and maintained momentum, but his story is the exception rather than the rule. For the most part, the people I spoke to chose their subject or business and became specialists in it.

The Bruce Lee syndrome:

I remember a karate teacher once explaining how frustrated he became with new students in his class who became bored with the same drills and wanted to learn more complicated moves after only a few weeks. He wanted them to focus on the six fundamental moves that he was teaching them and said, "If they would practise six simple actions, ten thousand times, they would be masters, but instead of practising six moves ten thousand times, they want to practise ten thousand moves six times." The teacher is now wary of taking on beginners, especially those who say they were inspired to join after watching a Bruce Lee movie! In karate it is the fundamentals that make the difference, and the same is true in life.

Become an Expert:

Personal Best People: Indro Mukerjee - CEO Plastic Logic
"You have to specialise. As markets become more and more competitive, you have to find a unique edge that you or your business can offer."

Ultimately, if you want to increase your worth, your knowledge or understanding, you have to become a specialist, an expert in your chosen area. Whatever area you choose, you need to commit to being the best in it, become completely focused on it, and immerse yourself in totally understanding your sector.

If we are to become experts, we can't only do something for a few days and then change tack and do something else. Achieving success at anything, whether it is a career or a goal, means staying focused on it for months or even years. I think we all understand this and when we watch the Olympic Games or listen to a great speaker, we instinctively understand they didn't become that good with only a few weeks' practice. The truth is that their skills have been honed over many years and their ability has been developed on the back of extreme focus.

To specialise means to concentrate on key areas without shutting yourself off from other learning opportunities. It is this ability to focus that will give you an advantage over your peers and your competitors; you become expert at what you focus upon. Effectively, if we can focus on one important goal and develop the single-mindedness needed to achieve it, we will become innovators and specialists in what we do.

Habits:

Focus is really no more than habit. When you sow a habit, which is simply a daily action, you effectively change the essence or the character of who you are and start to define the life that you will have. The power to habitually focus on the actions that you need to take will move you towards your goals. This is more than simply eliminating outside distractions. It is the art of self-discipline, of looking at your actions and learning to prioritise which are the most important to you.

Often the things that we do on a daily basis all seem necessary and it seems impossible to eliminate any of them from our busy lives.

It is the same for everyone. We make plans and then life just seems to happen. Other demands on our time or unforeseen events mean we do not get round to doing what we know we must. That it is why it is so important that we take time to prioritise whatever is going to take us towards our major purpose in life. What is going to help us to achieve our main goal? Keeping our eyes fixed firmly on the desired outcome and making difficult decisions, perhaps even disappointing other people from time to time, is a price that may need to be paid if our goals are to be achieved.

Focused individuals are not always easy to live with. When we strive for something it can become all-consuming. When we are trying to achieve something in our life, we can become so focused and driven that relationships, health and other aspects of our life can suffer. Clearly in the long term this is neither desirable nor sustainable, but occasionally, when a task needs to be completed, the ability to break through the tiredness, avoid distractions and do what would be easier not to do is what differentiates those who get what they want from those who do not.

Focus as ignition:

Realisable value comes from specialised knowledge and we need to be able to focus on the important tasks and ensure that they are carried out. When sunrays are focused through a magnifying glass, enough energy can be generated to set fire to a piece of paper. The same principle applies to life. Focus ignites life in new and exciting ways.

Personal Best People: Frank McKinney - Real Estate Rockstar and Bestselling Author
"Apply true focus to what you do best. Until you are ready, do not be distracted outside your niche."

Nobody likes to be labelled one-dimensional and in today's world it seems that we are rewarded for being able to multi-task and appearing to have a level of expertise in everything. But if we stay true to our own values and the things that we believe in we will develop an unshakeable foundation, based on our beliefs and knowledge. We become true specialists, rather than somebody who has a veneer of basic knowledge. Commitment and focus on our chosen area provides us with this specialist platform. It is this single-minded focus that has helped every successful person to achieve their goals.

GOOGLE

An example of maintaining focus is Google, a corporation which now has so many arms and subdivisions that it is unrecognisable from the business that it was just a few short years ago. The company continues to add to its services with products such as Google Mail, Google Earth, AdSense, Translation Services, Google Checkout and AdWords. Google has also moved into the software market by producing a rival to Microsoft's Office and is now even partnering with hardware companies in a bid to produce operating systems for tablets and mobiles. But despite all its innovation, Google still focuses on the thing that made it great; it still focuses on search. Fundamentally the company is committed to giving its users the best possible search engine experience and providing the most relevant results every time a keyword is entered into the Google window. Google's home page has remained clean and uncluttered. The company prides itself on its laser beam focus to be the best internet search tool on the market. It knows that this is what has made it successful and if it is to succeed in other areas, it must retain that focus on being the best at what made it great in the first place.

Maintaining focus:

Maintaining focus in the world today is more difficult than ever; email, internet, telephone, TV, and social networks are all potential distractions. We also have to juggle family life, personal relationships and our jobs, as well as outside interests and hobbies. It can be very difficult to remain focused on the important things in life, but it is absolutely necessary, both in our daily habits and in relation to our wider goals. Whatever career, business or sector you are involved in, whatever your major main purpose in life might be, you have to remain focused on it. Don't stray and don't become involved in other things. Focus on being great at the things that you want to be known as being great at.

Personal Best People: Cary Cooper - Singer/Songwriter
"I decided to push every door where there was even a crack of light. I was determined; I think that is the difference, when people don't see their dreams happening quickly enough they become discouraged. But I was so sure; I just went out with tunnel vision."

I spoke to a significant number of people who cited focus as a differentiating factor in their success and even when it wasn't articulated as focus, it was clear that there was an obsessiveness about what they did. It brings us back to their being passionate about their major purpose in life and the fact that it is easier to remain focused on that which we love. This is why having a clear purpose in our mind is so important to start with.

As we make our way through life, we can all become tired and distracted. There will always be something else to do and one of the lies that we tell ourselves is that we will get round to a certain task tomorrow or later in the week. We fall in to the trap of convincing ourselves that we have other, more pressing matters that need our attention. We persuade ourselves that before we do the task at hand, we have to run an errand, or speak to someone or reply to an email or read a relevant article. These are just lies that we tell ourselves to get out of doing the things we know we must do, and if we can instead enforce self-discipline so that we remain completely focused, day after day, our goals will become reality far faster.

Personal Best People: Yaro Starak - Founder entrepreneursjourney.com
"The 80/20 Rule had a huge impact on me early on. I'm still very much focused on a handful of things that give me the most satisfaction, and elimination of what does not. That's a guiding principle in my life, which helps keep things simple. It also makes it easier to be efficient as you only need to do a few things well to get the results you want."

Focus drives efficiencies:

Focus forces you to become efficient and more conscious of the value of your time. It is powerful because it pushes you into filtering out unnecessary tasks until you are able to intuitively evaluate whether or not a particular action helps you to move towards your goal, so that you can remove those that don't.

Personal Best People: Robert Edmiston - Chairman IM Group
"It is not the length of experience that counts but the intensity. You can learn more with six months in the trenches than one thousand years of filing. For me, clarity of thought beats hard work."

Being focused reminds you and those around you that if something isn't helping you to achieve your chief aim, sooner or later it will get shelved as unimportant. If it is not important to you, it is probably not worth your time. The ability to remain completely committed to something, even when it makes you unpopular, makes you exceptional. It makes you more efficient. Your time management improves. Meeting times reduce because you have realised that if something isn't serving you it has to be removed.

Focus and change:

Massive change calls for massive measures and when you want a major revolution in your life, you have to tap into your obsessiveness. Some people are obsessively focused when they start a business but as the years go on and they achieve all the things they wanted, they become distracted.

DONALD TRUMP

Donald Trump, the real estate mogul based in New York, tells the story of how he lost focus and the price he paid for it. Throughout the eighties he focused obsessively on his business, buying some of the most expensive real estate and office space in New York. He became a billionaire and national celebrity, was lauded in the press and began to do regular television interviews. Trump would attend society dinners almost every night; he championed community issues and causes, to the point that he eventually lost his focus on his business. He had started to leave the office early to pursue things that were not remotely connected to his core business, such as the Miss Universe contest. Trump tells the story of flying to Milan in a private jet to attend Milan fashion week without knowing why: it just seemed the sort of thing a billionaire should do.

In the early nineties a major recession hit America. Trump found his companies over-leveraged and bloated. The banks quickly lined up to demand the return of money which was secured on his now depreciating assets. Donald Trump was all but wiped out and teetered on the brink of bankruptcy. He can recall seeing a beggar on the street asking for spare change and thinking that compared to his own debt, the beggar was technically $900 million better off than he was. To his credit Trump turned the situation around, an achievement equal to that of building his empire in the first place. He also took a lesson from the experience and now stays focused. If you take your eye off the ball, you can perish.

Focus is a secret weapon that you can summon at any time. If you want to make a change in your life, feel the pain of being without whatever it is that you want, get excited about accomplishing the change and focus until it is achieved.

Strengths:

Many people miss one of the most important elements of being a specialist. It is the understanding of what your strengths are. We have already looked at how important it is to do something that we enjoy and this is also evident in the area of our expertise. We all know people who have niche areas of knowledge, people who can name every British monarch since 1066 or identify the main characters in each of Shakespeare's plays. Other people can strip down and rebuild a car engine; some can make your computer work even after a fatal error message. How do people get good at these things, even when it is unrelated to their main line of work? Usually because it interests them and consequently it plays to their strengths.

In 2007, a Gallup poll asked thousands of workers whether they felt that they had the opportunity to do what they did best in their workplace each day. Less than a third felt that they did and presumably the remainder believed their core talents were being wasted while they carried out unproductive work or did something at which they were not particularly adept.

Your strengths not only contain your greatest opportunity for growth but will also probably be something that you enjoy doing. Many people get lost in the haze of convincing themselves that by working on their weaknesses, they will become more balanced or well-rounded individuals. Although it can help to a degree, this process of shoring up weakness also denies you the time to develop your strengths into world-class expertise.

Personal Best People: Ali Lukies - CEO Monitise Plc
"In any business you need hill finders and hill climbers. The hill finders are the people with broad strategic vision, the hill climbers are the people who can make it happen."

Your strengths are the things which you enjoy; time seems to move faster when you are lost in the process of doing something that engages you. It also allows you to enjoy the experience more and improves your efficiency.

Our strengths are usually, but not always, found in the things that we are passionate about. The key questions to ask yourself are: what knowledge do you have that others would value? What are you skilled at? What are you better than others at? What do you do best? The last key question is one to ask of co-workers and your manager. It is this: if you could improve one of your skills to the point of excellence, which one would have the greatest impact on your career and offer the greatest value to others? Understanding this can give you vital insights into being a specialist. Becoming a specialist means working to your strengths, finding ways of pinpointing what you are good at and becoming even better.

Your Strongest Gift:

Our strengths almost invariably lie in the things that give us the most satisfaction in our life. No matter what we do, working should give us professional and personal satisfaction. If we live life from the perspective of loving what we do, then we will find that we will have a far more fulfilling life. Ironically, the things that make us seem successful to other people are not always the things that fulfil us. In our culture, we get rewarded for doing what others want us to do. This happens throughout our lives. We may be rewarded financially, by public recognition, a promotion at work or gold stars at school, for successfully doing something we might not have particularly wanted to do in the first place.

Many people who run a profitable business feel trapped by it; they don't feel successful despite having a vibrant business and would prefer to be out of it. The difficulty that they face is making a change; they feel that it is all they know and they are unable to move away from it. In their mind, there are insurmountable emotional or financial hurdles. Other people live a script, believing that they should be in a certain career, despite it not being their true strength or calling. They can do it, but it squeezes the juice out of them; it doesn't serve their life's purpose. Just because you love to cook, it doesn't automatically follow that you should open a restaurant.

Personal Best People: Julian Richer - Chairman Richer Sounds
"A lot of my job is generating ideas. I may not always be in the office, but I think about the business all the time. I see myself like one of those people who do the spinning plates on poles trick. I keep all the plates spinning. I hold the business together. Keep it moving. Keep it motivated."

So, where are your strengths? What is your strongest gift? What are you good at? Are you a creator? Can you develop products or ideas? Are you a good leader or manager? Can you develop strategies that move things in the right direction? Or are you an entrepreneur? Do you like to take risks? Do you like the uncertainty of a start-up operation and the challenge of building new businesses? Are you an organiser? Are you an expert in facilitating systems and protocols that make things run smoothly? Do you enjoy the responsibility of handling operations and do you have the discipline to imprint systems and methods of working on your organisation?

You may have elements of all of these traits in you, but most of us will have strengths in one of them. You may be able to come up with other skills than those above, but fundamentally, if we are to be successful we must identify our core strengths.

Personal Best People: Teresa Amabile - Professor Entrepreneurial Management at Harvard Business School.
"The best way to help people to maximise their creative potential is to allow them to do something they love."

Identifying our strengths doesn't mean that we have to be labelled with one unchanging description, or stuffed into a single defining pigeonhole for life, but part of the journey to becoming a specialist, someone who is acknowledged as having expertise in their field, is understanding what we love and what our strengths are. Usually there is a close correlation between the two. Our personal productivity and success is assured when we commit to being the best we can be in our chosen field and by combining this with a commitment to continuously get better at what we do.

CHAPTER 6: **Ongoing Improvement**

Improvement begins with I - Arnold H. Glasow

In all economies, income and revenue is determined by two primary factors, what we do and how well we do it. If we offer something distinctive and better than our competitors, we will have a massive advantage in any walk of life. Commitment to being the best we can be and offering excellence to those with whom we engage is a rare quality but it is a quality that many successful people have.

A key difference between individuals, organisations or groups is often that one group has set higher standards than the others. They have decided that they will become the best at whatever it is that they do and it is that commitment which propels them to achieve ever greater performances. People who achieve more have committed themselves to a programme of continual and ongoing improvement.

Personal Best People: Errol Kerr - Olympic Skier
"My motivation comes from the fact that I am not the best and as a person I am always striving to be better. I don't think perfection is reached or met but you can always wake up the next day and just try to do a little better."

As we discovered in the previous chapter, being an expert in our chosen field is important. However, developing our expertise of itself is not enough; in order to grow and develop we have to constantly raise our standards. When we commit to continuous improvement, we commit to becoming the very best we can be, and by doing so, we become the 'go to' person in our field, a person recognised as having a deep knowledge and skill base.

KAIZEN

When I visited the headquarters of Nissan Motor Manufacturing in Sunderland, I was given a tour of the factory. It is a sprawling facility on an almost eight hundred acre site, but the attention to detail throughout the facility is remarkable. At the end of the tour I was presented with a souvenir of a small plaque with two Japanese characters on it. The characters are pronounced 'kaizen', a Japanese word meaning 'ongoing improvement'.

Nissan United Kingdom encourages everybody within both the manufacturing and support facilities to seek out areas where improvements can be made to the business. The company believes that any improvement, no matter how small, will make a positive contribution. They believe that small improvements can reap huge results; by changing the location of a box, or how parts are delivered to an assembly point, productivity could be increased. When introduced throughout the whole business these small changes can have a profound impact.

Nissan have kaizen teams based in every department, teams that are specifically tasked with finding small improvements that will make a huge difference to the overall business. It interested me that the company took this commitment so seriously but it transpires that it is not unique to Nissan and many Japanese companies operate the same philosophy.

I was curious as to why Japanese companies in particular were so driven by this determination to continually improve, and thought that perhaps it was inherent in the Japanese character, in the same way that politeness and punctuality is valued in their culture. However, never-ending improvement turns out not to be a matter of culture but rather something that had been instigated to assist the country during its darkest period.

By the end of World War II, Japanese society had almost been totally destroyed and dismantled. The long war, culminating in the nuclear bombings of Nagasaki and Hiroshima, meant that the Japanese industrial infrastructure was almost non-existent; travelling was virtually impossible and even making a telephone call was difficult. America sent an expert called Homer Sarasohn to Japan to assist with the rebuilding of the country by implementing American-designed, cutting-edge management programmes.

Sarasohn recommended that the Japanese should also consult with W. Edwards Deming, a management expert based in Washington D.C. Beginning in 1950 and throughout the decade, Deming taught the Japanese how to improve product quality and reliability by applying statistical methods. His teachings on the most efficient way to build a sustainable manufacturing business model went against the accepted wisdom of the time. However, his lessons gave the Japanese a huge head start as the world recovered from the social and economic disaster of war.

Today, Deming is remembered and revered throughout Japan as the individual who had the greatest impact in helping the country to rebuild itself into an economic powerhouse that is world-renowned for producing quality products.

When we think of iconic Japanese brands such as Sony, Toyota or Nissan, we immediately think of high-quality, high-value products. Deming trained hundreds of engineers and managers in his basic ethos: improving quality will always reduce expense and increase productivity. This approach was quite contrary to that of most manufacturers of the time, who believed that improving quality would only increase overheads and reduce profits. Deming argued that even slight changes, if implemented correctly, could increase the productivity of each worker. If this productivity made each worker more productive by a dollar a day, in a workforce of ten thousand, more than three million dollars would be delivered onto the bottom line of the business, every year.

Deming's contribution and techniques became widespread in Japan. The combination of quality products and lower costs created a huge international demand for Japanese goods. Deming's teachings are now widely credited with introducing total quality management to the world. And the basic premise of total quality management is simply that a business can be improved exponentially by committing to small, consistent, ongoing improvements to the product and service.

Personal Best People: Julian Richer - Chairman, Richer Sounds
"I believe passionately in continuous improvement – the Japanese principle of kaizen. Improvement through learning is the cornerstone of civilisation after all and we should apply that to our businesses as well as ourselves. All organisations should be continually improving, which means continually looking for the best way of doing things. There is never a perfect way – there is only the best way until you find a better way."

Deming's approach meant that each worker became entirely responsible for the work that they produced and as a result quality control inspections were no longer required to achieve high quality products. This apparently simple concept pushed Japanese manufacturing to a new level. Japanese companies still compete each year to win the Deming Prize for contributions to quality advancement; previous winners have included Fuji, Hitachi, Nissan, Toyota, Mitsubishi and Matsushita.

Kaizen is continuous improvement:

We can all practise kaizen within our organisation, or on a personal level; by committing to the continued improvement of ourselves, our processes, our skills and constantly stretching in order to achieve just a little bit more. Kaizen doesn't require a huge amount of change to deliver results, but we have to grab and hold each gain to make the incremental steps which are key to major breakthroughs.

The ability to stretch a little further each day is something that we may need to work on. Success can be defined as growth and many of us are impeded by the belief that we are already achieving our optimum performance. This false mindset can hamper us and its roots can often be found in childhood, when well-meaning parents, teachers and peers endeavour to illustrate our limits.

ALL ABOUT EVE

Buccaneering entrepreneur Richard Branson is renowned as a daredevil both in business and in life. But he wasn't necessarily adventurous by nature. His mother Eve Branson was not a typical of a woman of her time. Eve had been a dancer and a flight attendant and had flown on some of the first commercial flights across the Atlantic. These flights were primitive by today's standards; oxygen masks were used in order to breathe when flying over mountains and at a time when most women stayed at home, Eve Branson learned to fly and joined the RAF cadets during the Second World War.

129

Branson's mother was clearly a spirited woman and when she had children, as well as being determined to give them a loving and supportive environment, she was also keen that they be self-reliant. To ensure that her son Richard did not become too dependent on her or lack mettle, she would send him on epic bike rides of fifty miles or more. On one occasion when he was four years old, she dropped him off many miles from home and told him to find his own way back through the fields of Devon.

Young Richard spent most of the afternoon chasing butterflies and it was only as darkness fell that he knocked on a farmer's door. The farmer contacted the Branson household where Branson's father had begun to rant and recriminate against his wife's foolish act. But instilling a sense of adventure was part of Eve's inheritance to Richard and when other mothers were telling their children to be careful, she would encourage him to climb trees standing below shouting, 'Higher, Richard, higher!'

Perhaps part of Branson's makeup and the reason he has built a multi-billion dollar, international empire of three hundred companies is part of that commitment to go higher; to improve every day and to discover what may be possible.

A commitment to grow:

Personal Best People: Mike Duke - CEO Wal-Mart
"There are three basic beliefs at Wal-Mart: respect for the individual, service to our customers and striving for excellence. Wal-Mart associates are hardworking people who have the customer in mind and are constantly striving to bring in new ideas for the company."

Ongoing improvement is simply a commitment to learning the skills and strategies that we need in order to progress in our own life.

Stanford professor Carol Dweck has researched the mindset and psychology of success for most of her career and her research refutes the idea that success is due to genetic ability. Her studies have shown that focusing on hard work, combined with a commitment to learn, delivers results. Dweck's research has shown that those who are open to growth will develop faster than their peers and that the only thing that stops someone's growth is having a fixed mindset which tells them they cannot go beyond their current parameters.

These theories and the detailed research behind them are quite startling and provide some eye-opening insights. Dweck's interest in the subject came from her time in school when those with the highest IQ were the only ones who were allowed to carry the flag in assembly, or sit near the front of the class. Dweck had always been near the top of the class, but she was uncomfortable about it and felt that she was only as good as her last exam. Even at a young age, she believed there had to be a better way of measuring intelligence.

The fixed and growth mindsets:

After earning a Bachelor degree from Columbia and becoming a Doctor in Psychology at Yale, Dweck went on to study the fixed theory of intelligence and focused on whether intelligence can or can't be expanded. Dweck and her colleague's research involved giving three hundred students a questionnaire which asked about their beliefs in relation to talent and IQ. They discovered that some students subscribed to the 'fixed mindset' model and believed that intelligence is a genetic gift. Other students, who believed that intelligence can be developed, were described as having a 'growth mindset'.

Once these differing core beliefs had been identified, Dweck set the students a series of problems. The first were relatively easy but they became progressively more difficult. As time went on and the students worked through these problems, Dweck began to notice something. The students who had a fixed mindset began to blame themselves, saying things such as, "I guess I am not smart enough," or commenting that they were not good at this type of problem. Some suggested that the instructions they had been given were wrong, while others began to complain about the environment, claiming it had become too noisy or too warm to concentrate. These were the very same students who, when the questions were a little easier, were answering them quickly and efficiently. Previously they had not questioned their own intelligence or complained about outside influences. Over two-thirds of the fixed mindset students showed deterioration in their ability to solve problems and most of them began to use completely ineffective methodologies in an attempt to reach the answers.

Dweck and her team then reviewed the results of the students identified as having a growth mindset. The most striking difference was that although they too, had struggled with the problems; they did not blame themselves or the environment. In fact, they did not blame anything or look for reasons for their failure. They simply understood that it was feedback and they would have to find a way around the problem. This more optimistic approach meant that more than eighty per cent of them continued to look for new ways of solving each problem by teaching themselves new strategies as they went along. Although they were no better at the original problems than the fixed mindset students, they ended up delivering a far higher level of overall performance, based on their belief that they could find a way of completing the task.

Personal Best People: Lord James McKay - Longest Serving Lord Chancellor
"Always do your best. Strive to make everything you do of the highest quality."

Dweck concluded that although some students may have had more skill within a certain problem-solving area, their academic talents were broadly similar. The difference in their performances lay in their mindset; those who succeeded had a growth mindset and were open to ongoing improvement. They achieved more based on belief rather than because of any inherent intelligence or skill. The group that had a growth mindset seemed to enjoy the challenge, readily accepted failure as feedback, and looked for alternative ways to grow through application and experience.

The myth of talent:

Many people look at others and see how gifted or talented they are; they believe that other people have an inherent ability to do something. However, the truth is that there is some genius in all of us. Conventional wisdom tells us that people are born with certain gifts, specific talents or that they inherit good genes and an ability to overcome limitations that the rest of us simply don't have. However, becoming talented is primarily down to mindset and intelligent practice.

Personal Best People: Nirmalya Kumar - Author and Professor of Marketing at London Business School
"Realising early on that I was not the smartest guy in the world really helped. It made it clear that to succeed I need to have a clear vision of what

I was trying to become and dogged persistence. I have a great work ethic which translated into coming to work every day by 6 am. This means I had, on average, a 2 to 2.5 hour head start on everyone else. They have to be a lot brighter than me to overcome this."

In the twentieth century, the world's violinists became better than at any other time in history; we know this because of a number of benchmarks, particularly some very difficult concertos, were reached. In the eighteenth century, it was generally agreed that these pieces of music were unplayable. But now they can routinely be heard at concerts. So what is the difference? It isn't that violinists are smarter or more talented. They have simply worked out how to achieve the dexterity needed to play these particular pieces, and they practise harder and smarter. It may not readily conform to how we like to look at talent, but research shows that those child prodigies who played the violin at a high level by the age of five or six rarely become professional musicians; and even fewer go on to play in the world's great venues. Why should this be?

Well, when research was carried out to try to resolve the question, it rather prosaically transpired that those who ultimately played at a world-class level were the musicians who practised harder and for longer hours. A second key difference was that they practised in an intelligent manner.

The power of intelligent practice:

Personal Best People: Pete Cowen - Golf coach to Major winners Padraig Harrington, Darren Clarke and Graeme McDowall
"The road to success is always under construction, it never ends."

When we examine how people excel, what becomes obvious is that they are committed to doing more of what matters. An elite level marathon runner does not just train for their event by running endless miles at the same speed. They introduce fast and slow miles, to reflect racing tactics and to condition their body to respond even when it is fatigued. A musician replays the same small piece of music over and over until it has been perfected, before moving on to the next one. A tennis player practises hitting the same spot on the court with their serve, hundreds of times in succession. We notice the results of constant practise but often misattribute this seemingly effortless success to natural talent.

THE BOYS FROM BRAZIL

When speaking to Simon Clifford, it is clear he is a man committed to ongoing improvement; he always has been. As a child he refused to go to nursery and his mother was forced to educate him at home. With this one-on-one education Simon was able to read and write before he was three and his tireless inquisitiveness meant that he developed an understanding of subjects long before his friends.

As a boy he enjoyed football and earned a place on the school team, where he excelled. His schoolboy career came to an abrupt halt however, when, during an inter schools match, Simon felt the team could perform better and were being hampered by their own coach's tactics. At half-time he communicated his opinion to the coach, who was also the headmaster of the school. Simon's view was dismissed and a short, heated debate followed, which resulted in Simon being substituted. He swore at the coach and as he took the walk of shame back to the dressing room, flicked a V-sign at the large number of students who were spectating at the side of the pitch, and was suspended from school as a consequence.

Simon decided that perhaps team sports were not for him and took up cross-country running; the tests of inner strength, resilience and self-reliance provided by the sport appealed to him. Simon was not content simply to do well, he wanted to excel and he dedicated himself to reading books on physiology in an effort to understand how he could make his body go faster. By the time he was eighteen he was able to complete a 10k race in thirty-one minutes, making him one of the fastest boys in his age group in the UK. Simon did not take the philosophy of constant improvement to the act of running alone. He also committed to educating himself on the very best training and nutritional programmes, so that as well as becoming a first class runner he was also his own coach. Despite his obvious ability, the head teacher that he had sworn at during the football match denied him a place in the cross-country team, a punishment that was never lifted.

The unrepentant teenager pressed on, and continued to get progressively faster. His determination to improve came to the fore once again when he decided that rather than just being one of the fastest boys in Britain, he would endeavour to become an Olympic champion. Based on his impressive results and by testing his own physiology, he studied what he would need to do in order to be able to perform at an Olympic standard. Simon was already running in excess of one hundred training miles each week, but when he compared his performances to the best in the world, he found that he was unlikely to become a truly world-class runner. Simon decided that if he couldn't medal at the Olympics, he did not want to continue. Simon could have run for his country but despite being one of the best runners in the UK, he made a conscious decision to give up competitive running. He explained it to me, saying "I felt that if I couldn't be the best in the world, I did not want to be anything at all." Having established through his performances and data analysis that he would be unlikely to be a gold medallist, he curtailed his running career. Despite this remarkable decision, his obsessive focus on improvement and research would feature again later in his life

Simon went to university and even though he had somewhat of a chequered school disciplinary record as a pupil, he was attracted to the teaching profession. Ironically, having qualified as a teacher, he ended up coaching the football team at his first school. The more involved he became in managing the team, the more he felt there had to be a better system of coaching. He wondered whether the talent hotbeds such as Argentina and Brazil in South America might offer some clues as to how the English game could be improved. He wrote a letter to this effect to the Football Association and received a somewhat curt reply, which summarily said there was no secret coaching or breakthrough methods being taught to Brazilian footballers, they simply had a lot of natural talent. However, Simon remained unconvinced that natural ability alone was the reason that the South Americans played with such finesse.

At around the same time Brazilian star Juninho had joined Middlesbrough Football Club, who were at the time playing in the top flight of English football. Middlesbrough was local to Simon and he and Juninho became close friends, spending time together discussing life in general and football in particular. With each passing conversation, Simon's doubts about Brazilian footballing success being based simply on natural talent grew. The more he learned about the way young Brazilians learned the game, the more he felt certain that current European coaching methods were inadequate. Simon began to understand how Brazilian boys really learned to play the game. For most people this information would have simply remained factual personal knowledge, and would not have been taken any further. But Simon felt that he had to find out more. He made the decision to go to Brazil, to study exactly what the kids there were being taught.

One can only imagine the conversation he had with his wife when he took a leave of absence from his work and borrowed five thousand pounds from the teacher's union in order to fund his trip.

He arrived in Brazil, armed with only a video camera and some notebooks and began to collate as much information as he could about the way the game was taught from the very early stages right up to youth level. At night he slept in grubby dormitories and during the day he spent time with Brazilian coaches, including legends such as Zico and Rivelino.

Simon's suspicion that the game was taught differently in South America was vindicated when he discovered that, far from the popular theory of Brazilian youngsters playing on sun-kissed beaches, they learned the game in the shanty towns they lived in. He said, "I found that Brazilian kids were not playing football on the beach. Many of the kids I saw lived in poverty; they played in the streets or in sports halls. But the difference was that they played a game called futebol de salão, which was a small-sided football game but with a far smaller and heavier ball than the kids in England would be playing with." This, Simon discovered, was critically important. If a player gets in a tight spot, the ball is too heavy to kick far away and the children Simon watched had learned to control and work their way out of tight spaces with the ball at their feet, as their only other possible alternative was to find a teammate to make a short pass to.

Simon identified this as the key difference between English players and the Brazilians who had dazzling close ball control and one-touch passing skills. In Britain most children were still playing on a full-sized pitch and many games resembled a Keystone Cops movie, with the ball being hammered from one end of the pitch to the other and a gang of youngsters running as a shoal after it.

Inspired, Simon came back to the UK and launched Brazilian Soccer Schools. The key to his plan was that not only would the English kids be forced into closer control with less chance to kick the ball away if they found themselves in a tight spot, but also they would have to touch the ball more times. The more they practised these skills, the better they became at football generally. The small, heavy ball used in futebol de salão demanded precise control and sharp, accurate passing. Brazilian kids were not just practising. By being obliged to touch the ball more, they were being forced to practise intelligently. Clifford says, "There was a mentality in England that we didn't have anything to learn, but I wanted to take the techniques I saw. The way that Brazilian kids played is that they used their feet quickly and it's the way you need to practise to master the skills. The kids I saw in Brazil had ability, but they weren't born with it. They learned it."

The Brazilian Soccer School's methods soon garnered results and he took a group of local boys who were not good enough to get a regular game with any of the Middlesbrough youth sides and created a virtually invincible team. The boys won games with such consummate ease that the BBC took an interest in Simon's work and filmed a documentary about what he had learned and the ideas that were being developed as a result. In the TV documentary, Simon's group of misfits beat Manchester United 13–1 and Liverpool boys 5–0.

The Brazilian Soccer School is now a successful global franchise and Simon's other venture 'Socatots' is set to become equally successful. Simon's obsessive focus and his determination to prove that a programme of ongoing improvement will deliver results, combined with his willingness to discover the story behind a story, have allowed him to develop a hugely successful platform. Perhaps in the future, it might even help England to regain some national pride in international football tournaments.

Simple commitments can lead to massive breakthroughs. The decision to improve a small area of our life each day has the potential to create incredible advances in our lives. Being the best we can be means asking a little bit more of ourselves in order to discover how high we can climb the tree of life. Whatever our interests or professional field of expertise, becoming great does not demand massive leaps in performance. But it does require consistent, continuous improvements, each and every day.

CHAPTER 7: **Nerve**

In case of fatal accident, I beg of the spectators not to feel sorry for me. I am a poor man, an orphan since the age of eleven, and I have suffered much. Death holds no terror for me. This record attempt is my way of expressing myself. If the doctors can do no more for me, please bury me by the side of the road where I have fallen. - A note carried in the pocket of French cyclist Jose Meiffret as he attempted a world speed record.

One of the challenges everybody faces when they are trying to achieve their goals is conquering fear, finding the courage to break through uncertainty to achieve the things that are dear to them. Fear is and always has been one of the greatest enemies of any endeavour. When Franklin D. Roosevelt said, "The only thing we have to fear is fear itself", he was speaking about fear as an emotion, for fear is simply that. It is not a physical manifestation of anything; it is simply a mental process that generates intense emotions.

People articulate this emotion as the fear of failure, the fear of pain, the fear of rejection, sometimes even the fear of success. No matter how far people travel on the journey of life, most of them are aware of this emotion from time to time. During the many interviews that I conducted, and regardless of the achievements of those I spoke to or how many personal dragons they had slayed, I found that almost everyone still had a fear or concerns about something in their life.

Fear can be useful. If we are about to cross the road and we see a bus coming towards us, the driver apparently oblivious to our presence, we simply don't have time to go into a stimulus response reaction. If we were to look at the bus and take time to think, 'Here comes a bus at high speed. I think I will be best served by stepping back on to the pavement until the bus has passed', we would be crushed. Fear is the fight or flight instinct that immediately makes us jump onto the pavement like a jack rabbit. Fear protects us and fear is something that we need in our lives – provided that we use it as a tool to serve us.

Sometimes the feeling of fear is well founded. If we are going into an examination and we do not have all the information that we need, then we may be fearful that we are about to be embarrassed. If we haven't completed our tax return and it is overdue, we could have a fear of the consequences. These emotions – and that is all that they are – are healthy and serve as a warning. They tell us that we need to become more informed, or more organised, to avoid pain.

Overcoming fear:

Personal Best People: Frank McKinney - Real Estate Rockstar and Bestselling Author
"Exercise your risk threshold – it is like a muscle the more you work it the stronger it becomes."

The fact is that overcoming fear is a skill. It is about developing the courage to face our fears. That does not mean that we become fearless, but that we have the inner intelligence to understand our fear and the ability to make it work for us.

Somebody who claims to be unafraid of anything is foolish; your goal is not to eliminate an emotion which on occasion can serve you, but to develop courage. As Mark Twain said, 'Courage is resistance to fear'. Our goal should be the mastery of fear, not absence of fear; fear is merely a state but it is an intense state. Fear has protected us since the beginning of time; it causes us to become more aware, more focused; it increases our heart rate and boosts our adrenaline levels. However, the problem occurs when we take this state called fear and mentally attach things to it that we do not need to have intense feelings about. You may have heard fear described as False Evidence Appearing Real, an acronym which reminds us that quite often the fear state is generated by something in our imagination. We hear a creak downstairs and think it is an axe murderer rather than the cat, or we learn that a colleague has been made redundant and rumours sweep the workplace as to who is next.

Take action:

Most of us at one time or another has felt fearful about something that never actually came to pass. We wasted time and energy tying ourselves in knots about the consequences of something that didn't even happen. Even when we are troubled by fear, there is a simple way to instantly diminish it. The greatest way around a fear is to take action and find the courage to move forward regardless of the fear that we feel. When a fire fighter runs into a burning building, does that mean he felt no fear? No, it simply means that he took action in the face of that fear; taking action is courage in motion.

Personal Best People: Craig Sams - Founder Green & Blacks Chocolate
"It's at night that worries keep me awake, so I just wake up, turn on the light, and scribble on my iPad or set out possible solutions to problems that are stressing me. Often that's when I have my best ideas, but even if they aren't that good, the demons have been exorcised and I go back to sleep."

Taking action despite fear is hugely powerful. Most of us can think back to an experience when we did just that, when we acted even though we felt fearful. What usually happens when we confront our fears is that they diminish, whereas when we seek to avoid what we fear, the fear grows and consumes our thoughts. If we allow this to happen, we find that these fears begin to control many aspects of our life.

Taking action conquers our fears and builds our self-confidence.

So what are you frightened of? What worries or concerns you? Do you have any nagging doubts about your abilities or life path? A common concern is the fear of failure.

Fear of failure:

Fear of failure can rear its head in any area of life – business, politics, sports or academia – and it affects adults and children alike. This fear is based on what will happen if things do not work out. What will the personal or financial cost be? What will other people think? Where will you go from that point? But before you ask those questions, you should ask: what is failure? What does it mean to you? What does it look like to you?

Personal Best People: Nick Friedman - Co-founder College Hunks Hauling Junk and one of Inc Magazine's Top 30 under 30 entrepreneurs "*I take calculated risks. If one idea fails, it's on to the next one. I never count a failed idea as an actual failure though, because there is a valuable lesson learned in each chance that I take, whether it works or not.*"

We must be aware that failure is just an interpretation, it is effectively only feedback. Just because a baby stumbles and falls when learning to walk, do we brand the child incompetent or a failure? Failure is how we learn. So if we change the way we think about failure and simply consider it a learning experience, what is there to worry about?

Look to learn:

You might be able to recall events in your own life when you didn't succeed or where something went wrong. These are the situations that provide our greatest moments of wisdom. When the winning team lifts the cup, they tend to party. The losers go back to the dressing room to ponder about what happened. It is during these moments of self-introspection that we gain some of our greatest insights. So what we need to do is to change the rules of how we look at outcomes.

This is not simply semantics. When speaking to people who have overachieved in their careers or their personal lives I noticed how they talked about events that had caused them pain. These issues included childhood abuse, divorce, bankruptcy, being betrayed by those they considered friends and many other painful circumstances. The difference was in how these people responded to unwelcome situations. They weren't afraid to learn from the experiences. This is a powerful insight and something I would urge you to understand not just intellectually but emotionally.

They approached the situation by deciding that they had to adapt. They did not blame anyone, they did not swear vengeance, nor did they question their own competence. Each episode was used as an opportunity to grow. This does not mean that they were happy with what was happening at the time, but every one of them seemed to recover quickly and recognise the benefits that the situation might afford them. This is the key. Regardless of how a situation may be viewed from an objective basis, these achievers only looked at the positive side of what had happened. This is critical. These intelligent, measured, empathetic men and women blinkered themselves to the pain and inconvenience and focused exclusively on the opportunity.

Take an example. We might be worried about fear of loss, such as the loss of money or the loss of emotional investment in a relationship, especially if we are fearful of other people's opinions. But if we changed our approach to: 'if this works out, I will achieve my goal but even if it doesn't, I will still learn something', the fear simply disappears. It is just a case of changing the rules of our internal game. If we win, we win but if we do not, we still come away with valuable insight, experience and knowledge. This means that we can feel good about success but also feel good about the learning process that failure provides.

This is not dumb or Pollyanna-type thinking. This is important. These are the rules for our lives. If our rules say that unless we earn a million pounds a year, we are a failure, then earning nine hundred and ninety thousand pounds a year will not be good enough for us and we will not feel good. We will feel that we have failed. However, if we can get into a state that allows us to intelligently extract good from every situation, we will feel good when we achieve our goals and hit our number and when we don't, we can still feel good about gathering information that will assist us to become better.

If a high jumper preparing for the Olympics bursts into tears every time he or she fails to clear the bar in training, their career will be a short one. It would be brought to a halt by the emotional intensity of daily failure. Instead, if every time they make a mistake on a jump, they draw on the lesson, make a slight alteration – how they angle their body, the way they run into the wind, the exact spot to take off from – they will get better at what they do.

Brendan and Johnny

Johnny Nelson first joined the gym simply to find some new friends. He was tired of hanging around street corners and there wasn't much else to do in the city of Sheffield where he lived. Brendan Ingle was an experienced boxing coach who had developed the careers of a number of professional boxers. Johnny joined Brendan's gym despite having no desire box. He liked the idea of keeping fit and working out, but he had no interest in being hit; he had been involved in fights at school and he had not liked it. In fact, Johnny was frightened to fight.

Young Johnny enjoyed the camaraderie of the boxing gym but studiously avoided sparring with anyone. He preferred to lift weights and vent whatever frustrations he had on the punch bags. As time wore on, however, he was cajoled, teased and pressured by his peers into doing some light sparring. In order to protect everyone, Brendan only allowed strikes to the body so Johnny reluctantly agreed to give it a go. Sadly, his fear of getting hurt meant that he was unable to adequately defend himself and he was badly beaten. Although he tried to do better each week, it only got worse as his anxieties thwarted his good intentions. He felt hurt and frustrated and many times he would go home on the bus quietly sobbing, but it did not occur to him to give up. He just became determined to become stronger. Even though he was frightened he was not a coward, and he had a stubborn streak which prevented him from quitting.

As the months became years, Johnny became a fairly adept boxer. He was no longer the easy mark at the gym and he could spar adequately with some excellent boxers. But he was still the only boxer at the gym not to fight in competitions. Sparring was one thing but fighting in front of an audience was quite another. When he turned seventeen, the age by which most boxers have had a long amateur career and would be considering turning professional, Brendan suggested to Johnny that perhaps it was time to try his hand at a couple of amateur fights. Johnny still had no motivation to hit anyone and was hugely driven not to be hit himself but he trusted Brendan as another boy might trust his father. "OK," he said. "I'll give it a go." It was going to be an interesting journey.

Johnny had thirteen amateur fights, most of them against men who were older than him. He took an instant dislike to it but he wouldn't give up. He would sometimes sit in the dressing room and pray that his opponent wouldn't show up, thereby saving them both the trouble of fighting. Johnny still remembers the palpable fear of eyeing opponents across the ring and being scared of the damage that could be done to him. The other thing he can still remember is that even when he was being beaten regularly, his pride wouldn't allow him to go down. Sometimes it would have been easier to take a dive, listen to the count and just get out of the ring, but he wouldn't do it. For all the hurt and fear that he felt, even at times when he was knocked semiconscious, he didn't slump to the ground; he would always try to hang on to the ropes, or his opponent or even the referee, anything to stay on his feet. Johnny only won three of his thirteen fights and his boxing career appeared to be on a less than stellar trajectory. He was also disqualified twice, once for not being willing to hit his opponent and the other for holding his opponent while watching the clock run down.

When Johnny left school, he took a few menial jobs but soon found himself unemployed and in desperate need of an income. Incredibly, his career choice was to become a professional boxer. He had discovered that after deducting his expenses he could earn about £150 per fight. It was not much of an income, but better than the wage he had been paid in a burger restaurant. It came as a surprise to nobody that he lost his first three professional bouts. Johnny knew that if he always lost he would not be able to get any fights and so, torn between money and fear, he developed a style of boxing that enabled him to win a number of points victories, without getting hurt. He refined this hit-and-move style and it served him reasonably well for the next few years.

Four years after turning professional, Johnny was given the chance to fight for the WBC Cruiserweight title. In the previous year, he had been able to beat some credible opponents and this was his chance to shine against an ageing Carlos De León. The champion had lost his old sparkle and with the fight due to take place in Sheffield, everybody favoured Johnny to win – everybody except Johnny himself. All his old doubts came flooding back and despite the fight being held in his home city, he felt nothing but fear. On the night, he barely threw a punch. The bout was generously called a draw but De León kept the world crown and Johnny was booed from the ring by his own fans. He had never felt lower in his life.

He took a day to reflect on what had happened and decided that he wanted another bout as soon as possible in order to obliterate the memory of the fear he had shown. His next opponent was Dino Homsey, who arrived in the ring with a red rose and blew Johnny a kiss; the crowd roared its collective approval, such was the level of apathy and ridicule that Johnny now attracted. But Johnny beat Homsey and he also went on to win his next few fights. Despite this, he still felt that he had blown his chance; he was still a laughing stock in Sheffield, following his Bambi-like performance against De Leon.

Things turned around for Johnny on the day that Brendan Ingle put an advert in the local paper to find sparring partners. Johnny was now considered so irrelevant that his manager was struggling to find fighters for him to train with. Brendan offered to pay a hundred pounds to anybody who thought they could fill the role. The pubs were full of men boasting that they could have done better than Nelson had during his championship bout, so here was their chance to prove it. A hundred pounds a day was offered and a two hundred pound bonus if they lasted a full week. Brendan did not tell Johnny of his plan.

The following Sunday, Johnny arrived at the gym as usual and found cars parked on both sides of what was usually an empty street. When he went inside the gym, it was crowded with people, some of whom he knew and had considered friends. What soon became clear was that the rabble were relishing the chance of knocking him out or at the very least earning some easy money.

Brendan's masterstroke went further. He stood in the middle of the gym and thanked the men for coming; he then reached into his pocket and produced a letter. He had received several of these letters, all of which were laden with expletives and abuse directed at Johnny and accusing him of cowardice, fear and ineptitude. The letters were abusive both to him personally and to his family. One even contained three white feathers, synonymous with those thrown at 'conscription-dodgers' accused of cowardice during the war. Ingle shouted out across the gym, "Does anybody know who sent these?" The atmosphere in the gym grew heavy.

Johnny fumbled blindly in his kit bag; he was embarrassed, and angry with Ingle for not telling him about the letters. Then a man came forward and said, "I wrote that letter and I'll tell you why. Because it's true! He is a coward; my wife suggested I come here today to earn a few quid so we can buy some new furniture." The speaker eyed the boxer and Brendan suggested that he be the first to spar with Johnny. The ordinarily even-tempered Johnny despatched his first opponent with three blows. Maybe he had not covered himself in glory during the world title bout, but he was a professionally trained fighter. After seeing the fate of the first challenger, the remaining men quickly slunk away.

That anger stayed with Johnny Nelson for years. It not only helped to rid him of his fear, but it also gave him the strength to believe that he would never again allow fear to deny him becoming the best that he could be. After many years and a series of impressive wins, Johnny was back in contention for a world title shot and finally, in 1999, a full nine years after the De León debacle, Johnny fought Carl Thompson for the WBO Cruiserweight title. After suffering nine years of ridicule, of having to re-earn his credibility, Johnny took his opportunity and won the fight on a technical knockout. Johnny Nelson is remembered as one of Britain's most successful fighters; he was undefeated throughout the remainder of his career and held the World Cruiserweight Championship for five years.

It was the anger and the determination to never again feel the way he did on that Sunday morning that motivated Johnny Nelson to take massive, unrelenting action and to face his fears one fight at a time. The masterstroke that Brendan Ingle played gave him the fire in his belly to go on to be a successful fighter and fulfil his potential. You and I may not need to physically fight for what we want, but we do need to stoke the flames of a compelling desire and learn how to take action despite fear.

The intelligence to take action and see each setback as a way of developing insights is perhaps the most powerful way of tackling fear or uncertainty in our lives. If we can reach a position where success is success and failure is simply feedback, then we never need to fear failure again.

Fear of success:

Strangely, fear can also manifest itself when we think of the success we might have in our lives and we start to worry about what people will think of us. Will they view us negatively? Will we able to keep the same friends? These fears are generally unfounded but we may find, that as we grow, we are obliged or want to leave some things behind.

We may change our workplace; spend less time with certain friends and more time with others. Perhaps we will move house or location. Sometimes these changes, despite being progressive, evoke the spectre of fear or uncertainty about the unknown. The fear of success can manifest as self-sabotage which needs to be defended against. It can be difficult to recognise, but this fear should be dealt with in the same way as any other: take intelligent action and commit to the experience.

Personal Best People: Sir Michael Smurfit - former Chairman Smurfit Group

"As a young man, I decided to leave my father's business and the day I was due to emigrate, I was hospitalised with a serious illness. The friend I was due to emigrate with went ahead on the trip and was killed at a bus stop not long after he arrived. This experience had an effect on me. I learned never to fear risk. Taking over companies can be risky but the disease I had was TB; it could have killed me or I could have been unfortunate like my friend. So nothing is that risky in comparison."

Fear of loss:

The other great cause of fear is the fear of loss or of consequence. We may fear losing our jobs or losing a loved one. The fear can be triggered by guilty feelings; for example if you have stepped outside a boundary of the standards that you usually set for yourself and are concerned about a resulting punishment for your actions, you may feel fear as a consequence. This brings us back to fear being an emotion. In essence, it is simply the anticipation that you may need to prepare for something. It is entirely positive to feel the fear when there is a good reason for it. Heed it as a warning; use the fear to understand the situation and prepare for it.

The Fear Extinguisher:

Personal Best People: Lord Paddy Ashdown - former Liberal Party Leader
"I have taken a lot of risks, some of them very foolish, but in the end, they seem to have worked out as well or better than I had any right to expect."

The way to handle fear is with massive, intelligent action and once the action has been taken, we simply need to believe that things will turn out in the best possible way. Once we have done all that we can do to deal with a particular situation, the most intelligent action that we can take is to simply get on with life. We have done everything we can to prepare and the truth is that most fears rarely come to anything.

Take a moment right now to list the primary fears that have held you back in the past. The first question to ask yourself is: what are you afraid of? Once you have done that, ask yourself, 'Why am I afraid of it?' and 'What consequence do I anticipate if what I fear actually comes to pass?' Then ask yourself, 'How does this fear hold me back in life?' and 'How does this fear limit me?'

Now be honest and ask yourself: in what ways does the fear help you? That might seem a strange question but there are two elements to it. The first is to ask what warning the fear is giving you. What can you intelligently learn from it? And the second is what excuse does the fear give you to get out of doing the things that you know you must do? Be brutally honest and finally ask, 'What would I be able to do if I get rid of this fear?' Throughout this book we have looked at how asking intelligent questions can deliver intelligent answers, and dealing with fear is no exception.

Remember: whatever you focus on is invariably what will turn up in your life. If you focus on a wonderful, abundant life filled with the things that you want, and you hold that picture in your mind consistently, then invariably that is what will turn up in your life. Equally, if you hold images of that which you fear most, those fears may manifest. So keep a guard on your mind and keep your focus on the things that support you in being the person that you want to become.

As we will see from the next chapter, action is everything and by taking action each day we will get rid of our fears. I am endeavouring to communicate the collective wisdom of hundreds of high achievers in this book. If you were to sit down with all of them, they would each tell you a story of how they had to confront their fear, how they had to act almost against their own will in order to move forward. Courage is nothing more than acting in the face of fear and your fears are no more powerful than the associations that you link to them.

So take action. Enjoy your success as success and consider any dips that you may encounter in the road as feedback.

CHAPTER 8: **Action**

The heights by great men reached and kept were not attained by sudden flight, but they, while their companions slept, were toiling upward in the night. - Henry Wadsworth Longfellow

Action doesn't just speak louder than words, it speaks louder than everything. Intelligent, consistent action delivers massive results. Everybody I spoke to while researching the key traits of success, regardless of the field they were involved in, had taken massive action to realise their goals and aspirations. Many of us get bogged down procrastinating; we spend more energy worrying about what has to be done than actually doing it. All of our planning, research and strategy will count for nothing if we don't take action towards our goals.

Personal Best People: Simon Tucker - CEO SRT Plc
"The most valuable advice I could give to others is; Go for it. Everyone is presented with opportunities the difference between people is that some take them and some don't."

There are numerous ways to achieve what you want in life. By using some of the methods shown in the second half of this book you will find quicker ways to achieve your outcomes, more efficient methods and more effective strategies, but ultimately you have to take action. Dreaming and scheming has its place but you have to commit to acting on your desires to make them reality. Most of us have, at some point in our lives, not followed through on our ideas or put something off. You may have found this yourself with certain tasks that you don't enjoy. Think about your tax return for instance. Why do people wait until the last moment to get it filled in? Because the pain of doing it outweighs the pleasure of getting it done. Of course the reason for eventually completing it is because the pain of having a knock on the door from the local tax inspector is a whole lot less pleasurable. Students wait until the last moment before starting important homework assignments; people wait until they can no longer fit into their clothes before they join a gym. We accept that this is illogical, but we still do it. This is the pain–pleasure principle at work; we are motivated to move towards pleasure and away from pain, so we run continuous internal mental evaluations. We have to choose to go through the perceived pain of taking action versus the pleasure of doing something else and we balance this against the pain of consequence versus the pleasure of accomplishment.

There was an advertisement a number of years ago, by Nike, which said 'You either ran today or you didn't.' As someone who runs a bit, this resonated with me, because we can always find reasons not to do something. We can choose not to go for a run and excuse ourselves by attributing this decision to the fact that we were working late or we were too tired or felt muscle soreness and thought it best to rest up. But the truth is you either ran today or you didn't. Could we have run if someone had offered us a million pounds to do so? You bet. Suddenly time, tiredness and weariness would no longer be an issue. All we needed was the motivation to act. Every day we are faced with the same question about our most important goals. Did you take action towards your primary objectives? Put bluntly, you either took action towards your goal or you didn't. There is nothing wrong with having recreational time; in fact it is positively the right thing to do and something that you should build into your life. If you take a day off you should enjoy it. It is entirely appropriate to take the time to do the things that you want to and on occasion, if you stop to smell the flowers, there is no need to beat yourself up about it. But if you are serious about achieving what you want to in life, you cannot habitually avoid doing the daily tasks required of you to realise your goal. You need to take massive, relentless action towards your primary purpose. Hard work and diligence may not sound too sexy, especially in a world of instant celebrity and cyber millions, but the truth is that action and a solid work ethic beat talent every time.

Personal Best People: Lord Robin Butler - Cabinet Secretary to five Prime Ministers; Ted Heath, Harold Wilson, Margaret Thatcher, John Major and Tony Blair.
"Get up early, get to work and don't quit."

The people I spent time with, regardless of their background, showed a huge commitment to their work and consistently took actions that helped them to develop both personally and professionally. They may have shown some aptitude for the profession that they specialised in, but that's all it was – a basic aptitude. The skill they developed came through hard work and consistent action. You could argue that Shakespeare, Einstein and Michelangelo were particularly talented, but, as we discovered in the chapter on ongoing improvement, a commitment to being the best, the compunction to learn more and be more, is what truly makes the difference. Some core ability conceivably provides a basic advantage, but effort and diligence is what takes people from being good to being great.

I DO RUN RON I DO

I went to the Scottish capital, Edinburgh, to go for a run with Ron Hill, a former Olympic athlete who is probably as well-known now for his clothing brand, which caters to the needs of runners globally, as he is for his athletic exploits. Hill was twice an Olympian and at one time was regarded as the world's best marathoner, with a personal best of 02:09:28. He was the second man in history to break 02:10 and the first Briton to win the Boston Marathon. Hill won gold medals for Britain in the 1969 European championships and the following year at the 1970 Commonwealth Games. Ron Hill has never made any secret of his success. He is a believer in action; massive, unrelenting action. Remarkably for a man of seventy-three, Ron has not missed a single day's running since December 1964. At that time, he was establishing himself as a top runner and he committed himself to running every day (and for a long time twice a day) in order to realise his full potential. This incredible streak, of running every day for approaching fifty years, has meant that Hill has run through injury and illness, with his baseline criteria being that he must run at least one mile on any given day for it to count. During this period he has run through numerous strains, fractures and injuries. Once he broke his sternum in a car accident, but he still ran the following morning. He also ran after painful bunion surgery, when on crutches he hobbled for a mile in twenty-seven minutes. This somewhat obsessive nature is what powered Ron's massive success in athletics.

Ron Hill was an incredible athlete but interestingly, although he was regarded as Britain's best marathoner, there were others very close to him. Hill's rivals included men like Jim Alder, Willard Cox, Trevor Wright, Ian Thompson and Donald McGregor. All of these rivals were men who were capable of going under 2:15 for a marathon, which even today would be considered a world-class performance. When you look at the training logs of each of these men, it is immediately clear that all of them took massive action. They dedicated themselves to their training, every day, usually twice a day, regardless of where they were, and whatever the prevailing weather. These men's careers at the very top level ended in the early 1970s. By the early eighties, names such as Steve Jones, Charlie Spedding and Paul Evans were also adding to Britain's reputation as a country of long distance running excellence. Britain at this time was also producing truly world-class middle distance runners, with Sebastian Coe, Steve Ovett and Steve Cram among others, battling over world records. However, for British long distance running, that is where it ended. The talent hotbed seemed to dry up. With the notable exception of Mo Farah, who, after several poor seasons, moved with his young family to the USA, so that he could train under the renowned coach Alberto Salazar, no other British male runner has ranked anywhere near the top of the IAAF world rankings.

Lack of talent or lack of action?

Today, when you look at the performances required to qualify for any given Olympic athletic event, you will find that the sprint times, jump and throwing distances of forty years ago would simply not be good enough to make the Great Britain Olympic team today. That is to be expected, because performances progress. This is true throughout British athletics – with the exception of the men's marathon times where, remarkably, the situation is turned on its head.

The current crop of British marathon runners simply would not have made the Olympic team forty years ago. Comparing like-for-like results against times that Ron Hill and his peers were setting in the 1960s and 1970s, current times are actually slower. This drop in performance has been felt acutely within UK Athletics. London marathon race director David Bedford, himself an Olympic medal winner over ten thousand metres, said that he felt the reason for this decline was that UK athletes are simply not doing the training by putting in the distances required. Bedford's view is that this decline is down to a wholesale lack of action.

The emergence of African nations such as Kenya and Ethiopia in producing world-class runners has clouded the issue somewhat. Their success has been put down to genetics or to the fact that they live at a high altitude. All this might contribute to some degree to the emergence of East Africa as the world's hotbed of elite runners, but it doesn't explain away the fact that compared to like-for-like results from forty years ago, Britain's men are slower. Regardless of how the East Africans or any other nation is faring, British men are running slower than their predecessors did decades ago. And when you closely examine how the Kenyans and the Ethiopians are training, it turns out that they are doing exactly what the British men were doing in the 1960s and 1970s. The East Africans train beyond what anyone could expect; they are obsessively committed and run eye-watering weekly mileages

When I spoke to Ron Hill and his great rival Jim Alder, they both said that at their peak, they were running in excess of 120 miles per week. Bear in mind that both men had full-time jobs during their peak athletic years. Athletics was a purely amateur sport and sponsorship and central funding was unheard of. Yet, when we look at the rankings today, they simply do not compare. In 1970, Britain had four men in the top ten of the world marathon standings. Today, not one appears inside the top two hundred.

When the first London Marathon was organised in 1981, one of its chief aims was to promote and improve the overall standard of British marathon running. Over time, other aims such as charitable fundraising and getting people back into sport have been accomplished, but Britain's male marathon times have continued to decline. The race organiser David Bedford observed that it was down to how much training people were prepared to do. He said, rather starkly, "I do not think there is sufficient commitment." Ron Hill explained that his golden rule is 'to train hard and get to the start line. Commit to training and commit to racing'. He feels that too many elite runners avoid racing; they are reluctant to test themselves regularly in the furnace of competition. He said, "If you will not go to the start line, you will never win or achieve anything in marathon running or in life." The lesson is that whether you are running a marathon or participating in the race of life, big action delivers big results.

Take action:

Personal Best People: Lord David Alton - Human Rights Campaigner &
Author
"Don't try to be something. Try to do something."

The strength of your purpose is what will drive your actions. There may be times when you are working hard without seemingly making much progress and you find yourself asking, 'Is it worth the effort? Will it pay off?' The truth is that your greatest dreams, or your best ideas, won't count for anything unless you act upon them and unless you work supremely hard to make them happen. It may mean getting up early and going to bed late, it may mean pushing yourself harder than you ever have before, it may mean handling disappointment and rejection. But if you truly want to see your goals become reality, you have to move through these challenges and doubts.

You can dispel all uncertainty through the simple step of taking action. Doing something, doing anything, is almost always better than doing nothing. Rather than allow yourself to become paralysed by fear and locked into a cycle of procrastination, make the decision to get up every day and take steps that move you towards achieving the outcome that you want. This will pay dividends.

Taking some action, even if it is not always the absolutely correct action, is invariably better than inaction.

As we have already observed, we find it a lot easier to work hard when we are enjoying our work, but even when we are doing something that we are passionate about, there are times when we may tire. We lose the will to continue. The constant effort can, on occasion, make even the things we are passionate about seem troublesome. It is at those times more than ever that we need to dig in and find the energy to push on. The acts that we perform each day, the habits that we form, will help us to fulfil our destiny. I don't mean to be melodramatic when I say that. It is not particularly glamorous, it's not particularly innovative, but just doing the same thing every day, working towards your goal, making the call, writing what has to be written, taking some action, will make a difference.

THE MAVERICK

Frank McKinney arrived in Florida at the age of eighteen with just $50 in his pocket. His first job was at a country club where he dug bunkers on a golf course, this was hard work which started at 4a.m. each morning and continued throughout the day in oppressively hot conditions. Frank bounced around a few other menial jobs before he decided to employ the tennis skills he had learned in his early teens to set up a tennis coaching business. The coaching was successful and the personable Frank built a loyal customer base. Over the next few

170

years he saved enough money to put a modest deposit on a home. The property, located within a troubled neighbourhood, was beset by serious social issues with drug deals and drive-by shootings commonplace, but Frank believed that if he could create a safe environment, the property could be fixed up. His intuition was right; he fixed up this home and immediately sold it, banking $7000 in profit, a fortune to him at the time. Frank immediately decided that this is what he wanted to do. The money he could make from buying and selling property far outstripped what he could expect to earn in the tennis business and over the course of the next few months Frank wound this business down. Real estate became Frank's business and over the next six years he became an expert in identifying the potential of even the most run-down properties, skilfully upgrading them and selling them on.

One day, Frank saw a property located on the coast. It was a huge but almost derelict mansion with fantastic views of the ocean. The house was called Driftwood Dunes and was on the market for $775,000. This was far in excess of anything Frank had ever paid for a property, but he was convinced that this home could be restored to its former glory. He discussed the purchase with his wife Nilsa and she backed his judgment. Summoning up their courage, the couple sold every property and asset that they had. Frank ended up selling his car and even some of his clothes so that they could invest everything in making the building a truly great home. Frank told me, "I know to some people it might have seemed risky, but in my mind going from small homes to larger properties made sense. I didn't need a college education to understand the law of supply and demand in terms of prime ocean-front property."

For the next two years the McKinney's lived in a tiny studio apartment. Frank had to seek additional finance to cover the cost of upgrading Driftwood Dunes in to the property he envisioned that it could be. He took massive, unrelenting action. Even when there was extreme pressure brought to bear from banks and other financial institutions who demanded their money back, Frank worked exhaustively to find new ways of raising cash to complete the project. To a great degree Frank was acting simply on faith. This project was a far cry from the smaller properties that he had experience in developing and at times it looked as though he had traded all that he had earned on a project that might well turn out to be beyond his knowledge and capability. But Frank's persistence won through. Driftwood Dunes was completed and it was a truly magnificent oceanfront estate. It sold for $1.9 million. Frank banked the handsome profit and never went back to small fixer-uppers. Instead he focused on creating some of the most spectacular and unique homes in the world, all with multimillion dollar price tags. He designed some iconic homes in Florida, his creations now typically selling for between $10million and $50 million. He continually looks to innovate and the homes he has built have included unique features such as internal waterfalls, floating fireplaces, glass elevators, shark tanks, bowling alleys, aquarium ceilings, and casino rooms. His passion for building truly unique homes has seen the size of his projects grow, each one bigger and greater than the previous one, with one of his homes marketed at $135 million.

Frank's name is now synonymous with high specification dream homes and only a select number of people can afford the properties he builds. He is America's real estate rock star. He still wears his hair long, rides motorbikes and remains a maverick.

The Work Habit:

Frank points to a number of things that have contributed to his success. One of the most interesting is what he calls the 'work-pail approach'. What he means is that every day he packs his lunchbox and goes to work. The following day he does the same. And he continues to do this day after day. Bear in mind that Frank is now as wealthy as he could ever want to be, but he is in the habit of going to work and taking action. Frank believes this is the cornerstone of his success. He simply turns up every day and works diligently. He develops his ideas and his offers, carving his niche and continually develops his knowledge. Frank spoke of the mentality of some entrepreneurs who want to make a product or service, sell it in sixty days and hit the beach. As Frank says, "That is not how legacies are created."

Achieving greatness and being your best needs the essential quality of self-discipline. Although Frank now has a glamorous life, doing TV interviews, book signings and creating ever more lavish launch parties when releasing his homes on to the market, he still packs his lunchbox and goes to work every day. The essential ingredient to his success is to be found in his self-discipline, the temperance to keep to his work habit. Despite the other parts of his life and an increasingly heavy media schedule, Frank is still involved in creating each home, whether it is planning, purchasing or any other seemingly mundane part of the process. He appreciates that his work-pail approach to life is what has seen him along the way; the discipline to keep turning up and doing his job.

So why do some people, even though they have a real purpose in life, something they feel passionate about and something that they are adamant that they want to take action on, end up not following through? This self-sabotage is what we have already spoken about, the battle between pain and pleasure. We move away from pain and towards pleasure. However, there are times when, although it seems contradictory, we do not do something even although we know we will derive pleasure from the attainment of it. These illogical patterns come about when we think that the pain of taking action will outweigh the pleasure of achieving our goal. It is when we allow doubt and uncertainty to creep into our minds. It is when we question whether it is really worth all the effort, when we fear failing or imagine we might be wasting our time, or that we will look foolish in front of friends, family or colleagues.

Greatness can only be achieved through doing. People who excel take unrelenting, intelligent action. The high achievers that I spoke to were ordinary people who achieved extraordinary results because they were action-oriented. They tried something and if it worked, they did more of it. If it didn't they adapted their approach and tried again, and kept trying. They pushed themselves to act and once they had momentum, they kept going, sometimes in the wrong direction, but they continued to learn and kept doing something, anything, that they felt would take them towards their goal.

Smart questions give smart answers:

You have to ask yourself some fundamental questions. Remember, these are the distinctions, the questions that will dictate the quality of your life. You need to ask yourself what action you must take to achieve your goals. What is the first step you need to take? What people or circumstances do you need? What action could you take today? What do you need to do next week and next year to make what you want to happen, happen? By answering these critical questions you become clearer on what has to be done. Listing your actions is important, but you must never lose sight of the fact that more than anything you must act on these plans. Strategising, planning and researching all have their place, but above all you have to get out there and actually do something.

Personal Best People: Chris Guillbeau - Author of The Art of Non-Conformity

"Contrary to what you may hear from the latest self-help book, true success does not come from passive visualization or wishful thinking. It takes action, planning, and sacrifice. Like surfer-turned-songwriter Jack Johnson says in one of his coolest songs - Don't let your dreams be dreams. Make them real."

When people assert that they want to stop smoking, why do they continue? If they genuinely want to stop and readily acknowledge that it is harmful to their health, why do they keep lighting up? Again, it is pain v pleasure, the pain of craving a cigarette against the pleasure of their long term health. The immediacy of the craving outweighs the longer term health benefits, which means they do not have the required motivation. If they knew for a fact that the next time they lit up a cigarette it would blow their face off, they would give up cigarettes instantly. The pleasure of the cigarette would seem small when compared to the pain of facial combustion. Smoking would become unattractive and they would need no further persuading to stop.

Action and motivation:

The only thing stopping you achieving what you want to do right now is that you are not motivated. This means that either the vistas of achieving your goals are not attractive enough to you, or if they are, that you do not believe they will happen. It means you do not have belief in your outcome. You fear failure. If you knew for a fact that you would succeed no matter what you chose to do, you would follow through every time. But we have become fearful, because we worry that we won't get the reward for our efforts. We know how to handle fear; we just need to take action. That is not to say everything will work out first time every time, but sow the seed often enough and you will in time reap a harvest. If you move forward with the sense of belief and take intelligent action, you can achieve your goals.

The only reason you are not acting right now is because you are unsure. If you knew you would succeed, you would feel completely motivated. You know how to handle this uncertainty. You know how to handle any fear. We looked at that in the previous chapter: action dispels fear. If there is anything you should fear it is not achieving what you could. You are going to live and you are going to die. Whatever your religious beliefs, you know there is a time between birth and mortal death. That time should be filled with purpose. None of us knows how long or how short that time might be, so, how are you filling it? What acts are you taking? The acts that you commit will become the destiny you will live. You have to take action.

Action and choice:

For most of us, our personalities are set by the time we are five years old. We carry with us, sometimes for life, the messages we receive from our parents, teachers and from outside forces about what we can and cannot do. To maintain your forward momentum, you need to rid yourself of beliefs that do not serve you, especially those based on someone else's opinion. We often make important life choices based on our history, or worse, on that of someone else. It's time to acknowledge that our history does not equal our future. You have to write down what you are going to do and hold yourself to those commitments. Don't waiver, don't hesitate; even if you are not sure if you are doing the right thing, do something. Move towards your goal, be intelligent, listen to feedback and check that you are getting results. If you feel as though you are off target, recalibrate but keep your momentum going.

Personal Best People: Alan Edwards - CEO Outside Organisation. PR Advisor to David Bowie, Paul McCartney, Novak Djokovic
"Always follow up what you say with action, so your word is meaningful."

When I talked with hundreds of entrepreneurs, CEOs, politicians, sports people and leaders, it was clear that they all had a propensity for taking action. They made a decision, whether for right or wrong, and went with it. Actions are based on the decisions that you make and the decisions you make always come from the answers to the questions that you ask yourself. Asking yourself empowering questions means that you intuitively know the right steps to take to achieve your end.

The Story of the Devout Man:

There is a well-known tale of a very devout man whose house was endangered by a great flood. He went down on his knees and prayed to God, asking that he be saved. The floods kept coming and eventually water pushed through his front door. At that moment a young boy in a small canoe paddled past the man's house and suggested that he should join him and get to safety while there was time. The man said, "No son. I appreciate your offer, but I believe in God and I believe God will rescue me. You do not need to save me, but thank you."

A little while later, the waters had spread over the first floor of the house. The man sat halfway down the stairs looking at the rising waters and again he prayed. With all his might, he prayed to God that he be saved and not washed away with the flood. At that, he heard the unmistakable sound of a motorboat engine. He went upstairs and looked out of the upper window. A rescue boat had been travelling around the village and offered to take him and any vital possessions he might need to higher ground. He thanked the boatman but said, "I believe in God and I believe that God will save me. Be on your way and save somebody who really needs your help."

A couple of hours later the man was sitting on his roof, the entire house immersed in water. He clung on to his chimney as the water washed around his waist. Again he prayed with all his might that he might be saved. On hearing a boom above his head, he looked towards the sky, thinking it was the voice of God, but it wasn't. It was a helicopter. The pilot expertly hovered over him and the harness man winched himself down and offered his hand to the man. "My son," said the devout man, "I appreciate your putting yourself in harm's way for me, but God will save me." Unable to reach him, the helicopter eventually had to fly off. Sometime later, the man was washed off his roof and drowned. As he stood at the pearly gates, he said to Saint Peter, "I have always tried to live a devout life." St. Peter agreed. "You have and you will be welcome here in the kingdom of heaven."

"Then tell me, why is it God deserted me the only time I ever prayed for his help? During my whole life, I only ever prayed for others and for the world in general, that it might be a better place. This was the one time when I asked God to help me." St. Peter looked down at his tablet and said, "My son, did God not send you a canoe, a rescue boat and a helicopter?"

So remember, if you find yourself shipwrecked, pray to God by all means, but pick up the oars and row for the shore. Make taking action a habit. Every day do something, no matter how small, to move towards your goal. Write down your plan and work your plan. As I said before, it may not be glamorous, it is not cutting edge, it does not get you on the front page of the news, but doing the fundamentals, taking simple actions each and every day, will have a profound effect on your life and on those around you.

Personal Best People: Brian Bacon - Chairman and CEO of Oxford Leadership

"Be purposeful. Clarify your intentions and the values you choose to guide your choices, speech, actions and behaviour. This gives you focus."

Taking action means moving outside your comfort zone. It is the Personal Best philosophy in motion. Every day doing a little bit more, stretching yourself a little further. This repetition eventually gets into your subconscious and becomes a habit. If you are going to develop new habits, make sure they are positive ones that help you to take action towards your desired outcomes. People who succeed often have skills honed over years of practice. As individuals they can be innovative, intelligent and engaging, but fundamentally they all face the same challenges, the same issues and problems that the rest of us do. This is true in their business, family and personal lives. The difference is that successful people are better at resolving them because they take phenomenal action to achieve their ends.

Remember that constant actions, good or bad, become habit and your daily habits will become your destiny. This will become the life you experience. People who succeed take massive action, regardless of what else is happening, regardless of circumstance or economic turmoil. However tired they might be, they take action. You either took action today or you didn't. Only you know the answer.

CHAPTER 9: **Leadership**

If your actions inspire others to dream more, learn more, do more and become more, you are a leader. - John Quincy Adams

When we talk about leadership, we are usually referring to the ability to manage and lead teams of people within organisations, the ability to inspire and motivate. Whole books have been written about leadership; companies send their key executives on intensive leadership courses; academic studies, surveys and research have been focused on it. We can find articles on leadership in the business pages and in trade magazines. Leadership means different things to different people, depending on their profession, background or vocation and many people endeavour to cultivate a particular leadership style, becoming autocratic, democratic or on occasion narcissistic in their approach. The debate about what constitutes effective leadership merits a book of its own. The leadership that is of interest to us, in terms of our own performance, is a different kind of leadership, one that can be identified in many of the contributors to this book. One could argue it is the essence of leadership: self-leadership.

What is self-leadership?

Self-leadership or personal leadership is having the discipline to do the things that we must to become the people that we want to become. Self-leadership means understanding our personal drivers, it is all about being able to motivate ourselves and manage our own actions. If we can't do that, how can we expect to be able to do the same with teams of people? If we do not set a good example ourselves, how can we truly become good leaders? Why would anybody want to follow us?

Some people leave their homes is the morning wanting to change the world yet their kitchen is a mess. They want to change the world but they can't even change their own environment. They procrastinate and delay and worst of all they establish reasons and circumstances, usually imagined, as to why they are not doing what they know they should do. Self-leadership is having the ability to do that which must be done. Without it, you will never reach your full potential.

Personal Best People: Lynne Sedgmore - Executive Director 157 Group
"Listen more than you talk. Everyone has the potential to be a leader, including you. Never cover up your mistakes, know who you are and never ever tell a lie. Always treat everyone with genuine dignity and respect."

The many people who afforded me their time in contributing to Personal Best were open to discussing their lives, looking not only at where they had succeeded but also at mistakes they had made. All, in their own way, were strong leaders, not just of others, but of themselves. They reached that little bit more to be their best; they didn't make excuses and when they came across obstacles, they either found a way around them or made a way through them.

Personal integrity:

When we think about personal integrity, we think about the ability to tell the truth to other people, to be morally correct, to do the right thing, to treat people fairly and to be honest with others. This is hugely important and a fundamental component of any decent character, but when I talk about personal integrity, I'm speaking of being true to yourself; telling yourself the truth, not making excuses, being strong enough to question your own motives. Why do you do things? Why don't you do other things? Why do you mess up? Why do you bunk off when you know you should work?

We can all find excuses because our lives are busy. When we do not follow through as perhaps we should, we can rationalise it with the fact that we had to collect the kids from school, or we had to get a report finished, or we had to run an important errand. Remember the Nike advert from the previous chapter? 'You either ran today or you didn't'. Well, if you didn't that is okay. Maybe you just didn't want to, but be honest with yourself, don't make excuses. You either ran today or you didn't, you either worked well today or you didn't, you achieved what you set out to do or you didn't. Avoid making excuses in general, but avoid absolutely making excuses to yourself. If you cannot be true to yourself, you are not on the path of self-empowerment but on a downward spiral of self-delusion. If you question your actions and motives, if you are your own hardest task master, no one will ever have to do the job for you. Being your best in any walk of life is simply a case of asking more of yourself than anyone else reasonably would.

Personal Best People: Nick Jenkins - Director Hansei Australia
"Every day I've had to make small choices that seemed insignificant at the time but later turned out to have monumental consequences."

This ability to self-lead was central to the thinking of virtually everyone I interviewed. They took no nonsense from themselves and they seemed to understand their own peculiarities and motives. They could be a little self-analytical, even self-deprecating sometimes, but they were consistently truthful to themselves.

Self-leadership and change:

An important facet of personal leadership is the habit of noticing what things are not working for you as well as those that are, and making changes when necessary. These changes lead to growth and growth is ultimately where we find our greatest contentment. As a species, we look to progress and we only feel happy when we know that we are growing and expanding in new ways. It really is the human condition; it is the primary characteristic that separates us from the animal kingdom. No matter how rich you are, how healthy you are, how fit you are, how loving you are, how happy you feel, if you don't feel you are progressing in the areas that are important to you, you will start becoming unhappy. You won't find contentment unless you are expanding your personal universe and the small changes that you make in your life, the small disciplines that you adhere to, make the biggest differences. This quality of personal leadership could be called empowerment, that is to say self-empowerment; it gives you the ability to change and evolve as you have to, in order to grow.

Self-leadership & intelligent questions:

We have already looked at questions and how they define the quality of our lives; by consistently making key distinctions, by continually asking 'Is this working? What would make it better? What do I want? Why do I want it?' Asking yourself intelligent questions leads you towards intelligent conclusions, and self-leadership is centred on knowing that you are on the right path for yourself; that you are living a purpose-driven life.

Personal Best People: Lord Neil Kinnock - former Labour Leader
"All I can say is that to me, leadership meant taking responsibility and no good leader can ever ask or order others to do what they are not prepared to do, in terms of effort and hazard if not in terms of expertise. Leadership only becomes daring when you'd rather take the public risk of failing than face the private guilt of not trying, it becomes a matter of compulsion rather than a matter of courage."

Often the great things that you achieve in your life are the things that on reflection are bigger than yourself as an individual. When you look back on the experiences that made you happiest, the successes that you have had or joy you felt, you will usually find it was something you did with your family or as part of a team or in a collaborative manner with others. Even in situations where you achieved something by yourself, usually you will find that the best times to appreciate it were when you could share that success with others. The more success you achieve, the more happiness you spread, the more of both you will to want have in your life. This is what success is; it is growth and expansion in the areas that matter to you. Your personal development is the quickest and most direct way to achieve your results, so commit to becoming a great self-leader.

Whether you run a small business or are CEO of the largest company in the world, whether you manage a local youth football team or are coach of the national side, become the best you can be.

By being an excellent self-leader, you can become a first class leader of others. Rarely do we see good leaders who are themselves poorly disciplined, unmotivated or unable to control their own lives. Now and again there will be an outlier, somebody who has been over-promoted or an individual who gets a role because there wasn't an alternative, but they rarely last. The great leaders that we think of, for example Mandela, Thatcher or Richard Branson, are all people who have had the discipline to lead themselves first, to make tough decisions and to ask more of themselves than anybody else could conceivably ask of them. Their self-discipline and the standards they set were two of the key factors as to why others followed them.

Leaders who are admired have earned their respect and this is why strong self-leadership is so important. Being respected as a leader cannot be demanded; it can only be given by others when they consider you worthy of the honour. This is why leaders who have an incongruent approach to life are rarely respected by peers or subordinates. They 'talk the talk' but they don't 'walk the walk'. These double standards are immediately recognised and if you say one thing and do another, rarely will others willingly follow you.

Los 33

On the 5th August, 2010, the troubled San José copper mine in the heart of the Atacama Desert, Chile, suffered a significant cave-in. Thirty-three miners were trapped 2300 feet underground, nearly three miles from the mine's main entrance. The miners attempted to escape through a ventilation shaft, but the ladders required by mining safety standards were missing. The duty shift supervisor that day was Luis Urzua; he instantly recognised how serious the situation was and how difficult any rescue attempt might be. Luis gathered his men in a small space which they christened 'the refuge' and told them that to survive they had to become organised and to work together. Their meagre resources would have to be distributed and each man would have to do a task each day in order to ensure the ongoing survival of the group as a whole. The men had no idea if a rescue attempt had even begun; they had no contact with the outside world and no way of knowing whether a rescue dig was in action. Concern grew that even if a search team had begun to look for them, it could be targeting the wrong part of the mine. Days later the men still had no information to suggest that their rescue was imminent; as the days became weeks, death increasingly seemed the likely outcome of their predicament.

It was fully seventeen days before the first borehole reached the group. At least now they knew an operation was in progress, but even with this development one can only imagine how each man worried as he faced his own mortality. Somehow the men kept their unity and sanity for an astonishing sixty-nine days, which was the time it took rescuers to drill and case a shaft to reach the miners and to develop the single-person capsule that was to be used to winch each man to safety. The rescue was watched by a global TV audience. When the last miner, the leader Luis Urzua, emerged from the mine, the Chilean people and the world collectively celebrated.

Many of the miners who were trapped have since broken the pact of silence they originally agreed and have told stories of arguments, fighting and how they divided into smaller groups. Cannibalism was mooted should anyone die of natural causes, and some men talked of suicide. As the days passed the atmosphere became increasingly tense. It may have been that without the leadership of Luis, none of these men would have made it out alive. So what made Luis Urzua such a strong leader in these difficult circumstances? The first was reputation. As the mine shift leader, he was known to have handled situations previously and had a reputation for caring about his men. This proved useful when he tried to persuade the group that they would need to ration their food. Some of the miners believed they would be rescued within a couple of days, but Urzua knew better, realising how far beneath ground they were and how difficult any rescue attempt would be. He made each man pledge to eat only a small amount each day in order to make the rations last. He also gave each man a task. Some of these jobs were useful but the majority were fairly unnecessary. More than anything, Urzua was keeping the men occupied, distracting them from their perilous situation with activity.

Luis Urzua succeeded in keeping the men united. 'Los 33', as they came to be called, came out of the mine one by one, sixty-nine days after the cave-in. The fact that the group lived is testament to the leadership skills and intelligence of Luis Urzua. His ability to appeal to each man's higher purpose in getting back to their family, and his openness to democratic meetings which allowed every major decision to go to a vote, meant that he retained the respect and support of the group. In the direst of circumstances, men can become selfish and focus only on their personal survival. This doesn't make them bad characters, it is simply a human trait. At our most desperate we are capable of anything.

Luis Urzua's personal integrity and mindset ensured that each man was prepared to set aside his own personal needs and entrust Luis with his life. As the rescuers worked through the night to bring the miners up to the surface, Luis insisted on staying in the mine. The journey time for the capsule was a thirty minute round trip, fifteen minutes to reach the bottom of the shaft and another fifteen to bring up each man. During this critical, nerve-shredding, twenty-four hour period, Urzua kept watch on proceedings and saw every man to safety, before himself leaving the cave that could so easily have been his tomb. When he emerged from the rescue capsule he was greeted by Chilean President, Sebastian Pinera who told him, "You completed your duty, leaving last like a good captain. You are not the same after this and Chile will not be the same either."

On reflection, I think the core message conveyed to me by the high achievers I interviewed was that they were doers. They took charge of situations, they took action when needed. But they didn't do this because they craved the thrill of having control over others. Ultimately, power is not something to wield over others. Power is the ability to commit to excellence and to take action towards your personal goals, without the need for outside forces to make it happen for you. All of those I interviewed were disciplined enough to use their powers of leadership to progress every single day towards the outcomes that they had envisioned.

Personal Best People: Lord Philip Harris - Chairman Carpetright
"Know what you want and if it goes wrong, admit it and change it."

Being a strong leader is more than how you impact on others, it is also about having essential self-leadership qualities. Remember, in life you can be the example of what can be achieved – or a warning of what not to do. What we do every day, the actions that we take, shape the way in which people will view us.

THE PRICE OF LEADERSHIP

Between 1997 and 2010 the Labour Party held power in the UK for the longest period in their history, with Tony Blair and subsequently Gordon Brown holding the office of Prime Minister. Both men in their acceptance speeches gave credit to a previous Labour leader, Neil Kinnock. Welsh-born Kinnock's legacy was to bring a party, generally agreed to be unelectable, into political prominence. The journey that he had to take to achieve this meant that he was never to hold the highest office in the country himself. Instead he laid the path for others to follow.

Lord Kinnock, as he now is, was insistent that he should buy the coffees when I met him on an unseasonably warm October morning in the House of Lords tea room. Kinnock is genial and grounded. I spoke to him about his time as leader of the Labour Party, when he opposed one of the strongest Prime Ministers in the country's history in the form of Margaret Thatcher.

Kinnock took over in 1983 after Labour's disastrous general election result that year. The then leader, Michael Foot, resigned his position and Kinnock was left with a divided party which was dominated by those from the hard left and the militant wings. Kinnock knew that he had to alter the country's perception of the Labour Party and change its political standing to a centre-left position.

In doing this he made plenty of enemies within his own party and, to compound his difficulties, soon after he became leader the National Union of Miners began what was to be a long and fractious strike. Despite the disquieting voices, over the next three years Kinnock managed to distance the Labour Party from the more militant elements and Labour moved forward into the 1987 general election. The party was still generally regarded as left wing and suffered another defeat. Kinnock began his second period as opposition leader determined to drive through all other reforms that he knew were needed in order to have the party elected. However, a year after the general election defeat, he was challenged for the party leadership by Tony Benn. Kinnock rallied support and won a decisive victory which gave him a substantial support base within the party, but it was a distraction he could have done without.

Kinnock then made inroads into Conservative policies and throughout the late eighties, Labour rose in the opinion polls to be the party that was most likely to win power. In 1990, Conservative support had dropped dramatically and Labour seemed set to win a victory in the next general election. The Conservative Party, facing defeat, decided to rid themselves of their leader Margaret Thatcher and replaced her with John Major. Throughout 1991, Kinnock badgered Major to go the polls but warily Major waited until the last possible moment in April 1992.

Under the rejuvenated leadership of John Major and with the support of the mainstream media, the Conservatives scored a narrow victory and Kinnock subsequently resigned, having been the longest-serving opposition party leader in British political history. Soon after the Conservative victory, the party became mired in scandal, with stories of MP's personal lives, corruption and outside interests making the headlines. Five years later, in one of the biggest political landslides in history, Tony Blair led the Labour Party to a historic victory. Kinnock subsequently became an EU Commissioner overseeing many reforms, but his largest legacy is still that he led his party from being completely unelectable to being mainstream once more. This was at the cost of fighting many battles and suffering considerable personal anguish.

The Welshman told me, "A lot of stuff went on that was very painful, but you have to be strong. I am always concerned when I meet people who cultivate a personality of strength or of being tough. Growing up in Wales I saw people who were really tough, as tough as teak. They didn't make a show of it, but they had huge inner strength. I always admired that."

Neil Kinnock never did get to lead his country. He is now sanguine when he reflects on this. As a former rugby player he feels that he played the game as best he could and worked to the best of his abilities in the circumstances that he found himself in.

Leadership can be an immensely difficult discipline and on occasion it calls for self-sacrifice. Sometimes we are called to make strong decisions that are not popular, risking the wrath of enemies and friends alike. When Kinnock spoke of his humble background and Welsh heritage, he mentioned a phrase that he has held himself to throughout his life. It is 'chwarae teg', which means fair play. He feels that he played the political game honestly and to the best of his ability and even though he never became Prime Minister, he believes that he has no need to reproach himself. The same can be true for all of us. If we truly strive to be our best, we need never be critical of our efforts.

Self-leadership builds who you are:

Your self-leadership and consequently your ability to lead others is based on how you view yourself and the actions that you take. Your personal view of who you are, the labels that you attach to yourself, make up your identity. Sometimes people put on a veneer or try to appear to be something that they are not. But in our own minds, we all know what we are and who we are. We know our strengths and weaknesses; we know what we are capable of and what we fear. Building an identity is almost like building a belief system of who you are. You develop an expectation of what you should be able to achieve and this in turn creates the person that you become. Creating a strong identity, setting standards to adhere to, gives you the power to realise your own potential.

This is why it is important to be careful about the labels we put on ourselves, and keep a check on our internal dialogue. When you say, 'I am just this type of person' or 'I have never been any good at this' or 'I am just short-tempered', you create an identity for yourself. It might be time to assess your inner-self talk, those things that you say to yourself, because the identity you have is the mirror that you hold of yourself and it is the way that others perceive you.

Personal Best People: Charlotte Bray - Composer
"The most valuable advice I have been given, and perfect to pass on: Don't forget to impress and be the very best version of yourself."

Your identity is usually based on the experiences you have had and what has happened to you. Often this means that you create false impressions about your limits. Your life is not governed by your experiences but rather by your perception of your experiences. Your identity is in essence the decision you have made about who you are and what has happened to you. Whatever you label yourself is who you become.

How to become who you want to become:

You can change your identity in an instant. You can do it right now, simply by making the decision to be a leader and thereby starting to develop a new identity based on the person that you desire to become. Without necessarily looking into your past, you can create a strong foundation to being the person that you want to be in the future. So who are you?

Ask yourself that question in the present tense but base it on who you want to be in the future. Who are you? Project yourself into the future as to who you want to be. Often people simply say, 'Well, I am the Director of Sales' or 'I am the beauty queen of my town' or 'I am Catholic' or 'I am a father' or 'I am a drug addict', and they label themselves with what they are or what they think they are, based on who they have been. You are many things and you have different identities dependent on the various roles that you have in life. You may be a great manager, a dedicated mother, an empathetic counsellor, a loyal friend, an efficient shopper and reluctant dog walker all in the same day. One thing is for sure. You are more than one thing and you can be more than you currently are based on the labels that you stick on yourself. Give yourself the gift daily of assessing your identity based on your core values and the goals that you want to achieve.

The strength of conviction accorded by a strong sense of identity can carry you to greatness. It was said when the great orator Cicero spoke, people would say, "Listen to how well he speaks." But when the Greek statesman Demosthenes spoke they said, "Let us march!" You can become the type of person who receives a standing ovation when you speak, or you may be able to inspire your audience to follow you. By having discipline and a strong sense of identity, you naturally become a great leader of others, somebody who people are willing to follow. So work on yourself first. Decide on who you want to be and be that person every day. Your convictions, your values, your strong sense of self-identity will mark you out as a leader and provided you stay true to yourself and retain the discipline of self-leadership, you will find that the impact this will have on your life and on those around you, will be profound.

Personal Best People: John Adair - Chair United Nations Centre for Leadership

"The six most important words – I admit I made a mistake. The five most important words – I am proud of you. The four most important words – What is your opinion? The three most important words – If you please. The two most important words – Thank you. The one most important word – We. The least important word - I."

Once you are committed to leading your life based on the values of who you want to be and the things that you want to see happen, you create a future identity. By acting and conducting yourself in harmony with the new labels that you use to describe yourself, you will find that this is how others begin to perceive you. If you are living consistently in alignment with the person that you want to be, you act in a way that commands respect. By continually redefining who you are, you develop new levels of confidence, even when pursuing success in areas where you don't necessarily have experience.

Your identity does not have to be limited by what you have done before. The fact that you feel confident, the fact that you have a strong sense of self-leadership can carry you eighty per cent of the way there. The twenty per cent remaining might depend on skill. It might mean that you need to learn, study and understand something. But that strong sense of self-purpose, of self-confidence, the very embodiment of self-leadership, will take you further and get you there faster than you ever believed possible.

Response and ability:

Your life has limitless possibilities but the quality of it will be defined by your self-leadership, the way in which you conduct yourself and act consistently. When you make a commitment to lead a life based on the characteristics that you know you need to become fulfilled, you no longer need to be coaxed, cajoled or bullied into taking action. You become completely self-motivated and self-reliant. This self-reliance rests on having a tremendous sense of responsibility. And one way of understanding responsibility is to break it down into its component parts – response and ability. Your ability to respond. How you conduct yourself in response to changes in situations and circumstances as they happen, the character that you develop and your own self identity is how others will see you. Once you have decided who you want to be, based on the values that you hold dear, all you need do is simply keep moving towards becoming that person and living your life based on those convictions. In doing this you become a great self-leader and consequently a great leader in all areas of your life.

PART TWO: **BEST**

CHAPTER 10: **Belief**

Men often become what they believe themselves to be. If I believe I cannot do something, it makes me incapable of doing it. But when I believe I can, then I acquire the ability to do it even if I didn't have it in the beginning. - Mahatma Gandhi

Perhaps the most powerful factor that will determine the level of ongoing success in your life is the nature of your beliefs. Your beliefs about yourself and those around you. Your belief about what you can achieve and what is beyond you. Your beliefs about money, relationships and spirituality. Your beliefs will drive every decision you make. Beliefs are effectively our filter on life. They are the prism through which we view the world. It is the reason we believe ourselves to be skilled at some things but incapable of mastering others. Our beliefs can serve us and allow us to function in society. It is our beliefs that allow us to understand what is acceptable and what is not. Our beliefs dictate what we consider dangerous and what we think is safe. This filter that makes up our system of beliefs is powerful and can be very useful. It allows us to function in life and stops us endangering ourselves.

However, some beliefs that we carry with us are not as empowering. They could be beliefs that we have carried since childhood that aren't necessarily true. These limiting beliefs can stop us achieving what we want. Rather than working within a belief system based on what you have been told or on the experience of others, you can realise your personal power by controlling your beliefs. If you decide to change and direct your beliefs, you can take exponential steps to change things in your life. Beliefs are the most fundamental determinant of your success. Effectively, whatever we believe is what will feed our reality.

Personal Best People: Peter Bieler - CEO Media Funding and Infomercial Pioneer
"I was confident right from the start that I would make it work. I didn't know how and I didn't know which product would work, but I had belief in myself."

People who make breakthroughs or succeed in their chosen field believe absolutely that they have the ability to realise their goals. They don't think about or talk about other possibilities. The most remarkable thing I found when interviewing achievers was that it didn't particularly matter whether they had any evidence to support their beliefs; the extraordinary power of their belief did not rely on factual evidence. The majority of people I interviewed simply had a belief that the business they started would be successful, or that the purpose they were driven by was a righteous one. The fact that there was no foundation to those beliefs, no background, no experience, was seemingly irrelevant. They just believed in what they were doing and their beliefs became their reality.

Positive thinking and belief:

This is the difference between positive thinking and the feeling of knowing. I am not decrying the power of positive thinking and expectation, but belief is something entirely different. If you have a true sense of belief, it will become the difference between hoping your goals will be realised and knowing that they will be realised. When you embark on any new project in your life, you might hope things work out, but hope is a poor strategy when compared to unshakeable belief. The people who I spoke to, seemed almost to know that things would work out the way they wanted them to. At the risk of being repetitive, something that struck me time and again was that although their beliefs invariably had no foundation, they nevertheless manifested themselves in their lives.

The placebo principle:

We have all heard about the placebo effect of drugs, where someone believes that the drug they are taking is a powerful new way to combat their affliction, when it is no more than a sugar pill. The fact that they believe this pill is having a positive effect on them and is assisting them with their condition, is enough to aid recovery.

According to research done over the last twenty years, almost a third of all medical prescriptions are effectively placebos. These estimates and the research supporting them were published in the Evaluation & Health Professions journal. Studies determined that more than fifty per cent of doctors had routinely prescribed a low dose placebo drug to cure an ailment. More than ninety per cent of the recipients said that they found the placebo drug an effective treatment. So why then are billions of pounds spent on drugs if placebos seem to achieve similar results when treating patients? The primary reason is that even when placebos are used, the doctors are still prescribing some form of controlled medicine. This is simply because there is no point in prescribing a sugar pill outside of a controlled environment. The chances are that most patients will read the prescription and assume it will have no impact. Once they think this, they no longer believe the drug will benefit them and the spell is effectively broken.

Knowing this should not alarm you in any way. There is not some great conspiracy to hoodwink us as patients. The truth is that many doctors have come to realise that for a number of non-serious ailments, a placebo or low dose is every bit as effective as a full dose and they prescribe accordingly. The patient's belief system takes care of everything else.

Beliefs as a framework:

Our beliefs about ourselves and the world around us are incredibly strong. They are the filter through which every decision we make must pass. Our beliefs dictate our identity; what we love and what we aspire to. But how many beliefs do we have that do not serve us? How many times do we look at someone else and think that they got to their position through luck or because of having the right family background or connections? How often do we tell ourselves that we can't do something? Whatever you believe will be your reality. Whether you believe you can or cannot do something, you will almost always be proved right.

Personal Best People: Joasia Zakrzewski - Ultra Runner and World Championship Medallist
"At school I was told I was no good at sports and lost marks for not trying hard enough. So I only started running when I was in my thirties. It turns out I'm actually quite good at it."

The impact of belief:

No belief, of itself, is right or wrong, but each belief is either empowering or limiting. Your belief delivers a direct command to your nervous system, making it true for you; belief or the lack of it is the defining difference between the outcomes of optimists and pessimists. When people say that staying positive and keeping a bright disposition means that good things will show up in their life, this really is no more than a belief.

Personal Best People: Nick Friedman - Founder College Hunks Hauling Junk and one of Inc Magazine's Top 30 under 30 entrepreneurs
"The best piece of advice I can offer based on my own experience is whatever your dream is and no matter how you plan to get there, stay true to your original vision and that will carry you through to the end."

Beliefs are no more than ideas, but they are ideas that we feel certain are true. This is why people, for centuries, have waged war over ethnicity, territory and religion. They fight for what they believe in and against the beliefs of others. The power of belief can be used for good and for ill. It is sad to see cultures killing each other over whose God is the true one. This book does not offer any political or religious ideology, but it is important that it communicates the fact that beliefs are simply ideas of how things work or should work. It can serve you to look at your beliefs and decide which ones support you and which ones might be holding you back. The beliefs that you carry will have a direct and considerable impact on the world that you experience.

Throughout the last few centuries belief has been closely connected to religious movements and when we look at the power of prayer, whatever our religious persuasion the fact of the matter is that prayer seems to deliver results. People recover from serious illness or they manage to rid themselves of a lifelong addiction through the power of prayer. It is no more than faith; faith that the prayer will be answered. I am not here to debate the finer points of religious dogma but what I am saying is that a strong, powerful, unshakeable belief in anything, be it a religion, ourselves, our society, our country – whatever we have a belief about, if that belief is strong enough, that is what we will see. Belief is the lens through which you will interpret the world

Psychologist Mike McCullough completed a study on the power of religious belief. His research looked at numerous studies that kept track over time of people who had been asked about their religious convictions. It appears that the people who were non-religious simply died sooner than those who were religiously active. Believers lived an average of twenty-five to thirty per cent longer than non-believers. This is a significant difference and has since been confirmed by other research. So are we to accept that God literally helps believers to live longer? Perhaps and perhaps not; that is a matter for each person to decide. The real message is that the belief in a higher power and the conviction of a chosen faith helps people to live longer and healthier lives. Of course there could be other reasons for this. It may be that people who are religious are less likely to have unhealthy traits in their lives, such as casual sex, drinking or drug taking. Additionally believers are likely to conform to other society standards, such as regular health checks, dental care and maintaining a healthy diet. However, all of these traits are based on their belief and that belief gives them more reasons to lead their lives in a certain way.

JONATHAN EDWARDS

Olympic gold medallist and one time triple jump world record holder Jonathan Edwards was deeply religious and a devout Christian. Early in his career he refused to compete on a Sunday, until he eventually became comfortable in his own mind that he could do so with God's blessing. Up to that point, Edwards, who simply viewed his sport as a way of expressing God's power within him, missed several major championships because of this conviction.

On the day of Edwards' historic Olympic victory, he walked into the stadium and prayed silently to himself: "I place my destiny in Your hands. Do with me as You will." That afternoon he captured the gold medal, jumping an incredible seventeen metres and seventy-one centimetres. After retiring from international athletics, he appeared regularly on television as a commentator and also had a stint as a presenter on Songs of Praise, a religious TV programme. Remarkably for a man who had never hesitated to profess his faith and the many ways in which he drew strength from it, Edwards quit his Songs of Praise role after he began to have doubts about Christianity. He questioned some of his beliefs and the more he questioned, the more he stripped away the central planks of his faith. Eventually, Edwards had to admit to himself that he no longer believed in what he once did. He felt connected to the possibility of a higher power, but his belief in a Christian God had crumbled. He doubts whether he would have ever been as successful in athletics if, at that time, he had not believed strongly in God. He thinks that his sheer conviction that God was channelling his power through him meant that he was able to overachieve in his athletic endeavours.

Belief and certainty:

For most of us, our belief system supports us in our avoidance of pain and attraction to pleasure. The only reason any of us have a belief about anything, is that we have either decided it is too painful not to believe in it or that we derive some kind of pleasure from continuing our belief. The fact of the matter is that any belief we hold, any unshakeable belief, is driven by what we feel we know. It is a feeling of certainty.

Personal Best People: Brianna Glenn - Team USA World Championship Long Jumper

"I've learned to believe in myself regardless. That's regardless if I have the world's biggest cheerleading squad behind me or if I'm the only one on the entire planet that believes it's possible. Confidence in a sport like this is key and it has to come from within."

You may think that your spouse is entirely faithful to you and that you enjoy a loving relationship. This is a fantastic belief to have; it supports you in having a happy, rewarding relationship. But suppose one evening you discover a love letter on the doormat, seemingly from your spouse's lover, and you then went upstairs to find your partner gone, a suitcase missing and much of your loved one's clothing removed from the wardrobe. Would your belief then be as strong? If you were one hundred per cent certain a few moments before about your husband or wife's fidelity, where is that belief now? How would you feel about the quality of your relationship? What if, five minutes later, you heard a knock at the door and a decidedly sheepish-looking stranger told you that in their haste they had posted a private letter through the wrong door and asked if they could have it back? What then, if your spouse arrived home, suitcase in hand, having at last cleared out those unwanted clothes and taken them to the charity shop? Is the world suddenly a better place? Of course it is. We go through a roller-coaster of emotions based on our interpretation of events, not events as they actually are.

ROGER BANNISTER

The Iffley Road Track at Oxford University's sports club is where Roger Bannister became the first man to run a sub four-minute mile. Bannister had chased the goal for nearly two years, working to a specialised training regime. He and three other runners in the world were considered capable of running under four minutes, even though many in the media and those involved in competitive athletics had deemed it impossible. Bannister, who was a medical student, had a good knowledge of physiology and anatomy. He believed that he could achieve this historic mark and was under pressure to do so, mainly from his Australian rival John Landy, who also had designs on achieving a sub four-minute mile. Both men though, only had their belief to go on. Their best times sat nearly two seconds outside their target, which in athletic terms represents a substantial gap. Bannister had given some thought to what it would take to push that little harder. In a later interview he said, "The world record then was four minutes, one point four seconds, held by Sweden's Gunder Haegg. It had been stuck there for nine years, since 1945. It didn't seem logical to me, as a physiologist, that if you could run a mile in four minutes, one and a bit seconds, you couldn't break four minutes. But it had become a psychological as well as a physical barrier." Indeed, the Australian, John Landy, having done four minutes, two seconds on three occasions, is reported to have commented, "It's like a wall, I couldn't see the psychological side."

In May, 1954, one week after a failed run, Bannister managed to break the mythical four-minute mile, coming home in three minutes, fifty-nine point four seconds. This was a remarkable achievement and he was rightly lauded for his incredible feat. But what is even more remarkable is that within fifty-six days and after years of trying, John Landy went faster, not only going under four minutes, but also taking the world record. Not only that, but over the next twenty-four months, a dozen other athletes broke the four-minute mile barrier.

The power of belief:

The power of belief is indeed an incredible thing; as soon as one man had broken the four-minute barrier, other athletes across the world believed themselves capable of doing the same. Whatever you believe, likely as not, will become true in your life. Your beliefs really determine how much potential you will be able to tap into in your life. It is useful to examine your beliefs minutely. Do you believe you can be rich? Do you believe that you can find your perfect partner? Do you believe you are bad at mathematics or that you are a terrible artist? Change these beliefs and you alter your patterns and in turn create new ones.

Changing limiting beliefs:

The beliefs we hold can be changed almost instantly. All we need to do is create doubt in that belief. All of us have believed things in the past that we defended stoutly at the time, but are perhaps now embarrassed to admit that we ever believed in the first place. So if we understand that the beliefs we hold are driving the shape and destiny of our lives, how do we change a limiting belief? How do we embrace a new set of thinking that allows us to move forward? Just because we experience something new, that doesn't necessarily mean that we are going to experience a direct change in our belief system. New experiences only bring about change if they create doubt or if they result in us questioning those core beliefs. When we believe in something, fully and wholeheartedly, we tend not to second-guess or question it. So it follows that we can remove our limiting beliefs simply by questioning or doubting whether it is true.

If you believe that you cannot start that business right now because your kids are in college, or because you have a large mortgage, or because it is too risky, you are feeding into your mind rationalisations as to why you should not do what you feel in your gut that you should. The moment you start asking yourself more empowering questions about how you could do something, suddenly the belief that you can't start that business begins to dissolve a little. The more you question it, the more you can create doubt about that belief, and the more it begins to crumble. As with any belief, if you question it hard enough, you can switch it from a belief to simply a vague notion and from that to the point where you no longer believe what you once did. You can change a set of beliefs that justify in your mind why you can't do something, into a new set of beliefs that rationalise why you can.

As Jordan Belfort, the author of *The Wolf of Wall Street* remarks:

The only thing standing between you and your goal is the bullshit story you keep telling yourself as to why you can't achieve it.

The way that you can cement positive beliefs in your life, to create the lasting change that you want to see, is to develop conviction in them. Many of the people I spoke to didn't necessarily have a frame of reference or any particular reason for believing what they did. They simply developed a conviction that they would prevail or that what they were doing was the right thing. This is an additional layer of emotional intensity and can impact on any area of your life. How do we bring about this feeling of conviction? How do we bring about a feeling of unshakeable faith, the feeling that what we are doing is right and that things will turn out for us as we intend? We need to take any basic belief we want to hold and steadily reinforce that belief, step by step, by developing strong references.

Belief and motivation:

The more you think about your beliefs and the more you ask yourself why you want to act in line with your convictions, the more you will create an unstoppable momentum. The more you examine your motives, the more you will layer reference upon reference as to why your goals can actually be achieved. This is how belief is built. By continuing to ask yourself questions such as 'How will I feel when I accomplish this?' and 'What will it mean if I do not follow through on this?' you will create more belief in what you are doing and why you must continue.

Another useful tool for cementing beliefs, and for creating lasting change, is to create some form of pain and attach it to the event of not achieving what we want to. It is an irony that most of us will move away from pain quicker than we will move towards pleasure. For instance, if I gave you a short guide on how you could earn £10,000 per month from an easy-to-run online business, you would probably be motivated to read the manual. Maybe you would read it right away, or perhaps you would wait until you were home, or maybe you would put it aside for the weekend. Some people might never read it. However, if I told you that a thief had made off with your bank card, and was going to withdraw £10,000 from your account, you would become super-motivated to intervene. You would not let the matter rest until the weekend. You would call or go to your bank there and then, you would take massive action immediately. The pain of losing money actually motivates people quicker and faster than the pleasure of earning it. This is why you should list all the things that you will miss out on, all the pain you will feel if you do not achieve the things that you want to in life. These reasons and the perceived sense of loss will keep you motivated for the long term.

The key is to develop a sense of certainty around the beliefs that will support you and the life you want. When you develop these empowering beliefs and gather supporting references, you have a strong foundation on which to build your life. So to change your beliefs, you need only look within yourself and decide what is important to you. What will happen if you don't change your beliefs? What pain will it cause you and your family? What will you miss out on? What will you not experience? When you know this, you are developing huge reasons supporting your need to change. The flip side, of course, is you can ask the same questions in reverse. If you get rid of limiting beliefs and instead adopt empowering beliefs, what will come into your life? What will start working for you? What will you enjoy? What will you see? Who will you be with? What will you experience?

Creating a new belief platform:

Taking the development of a belief system a stage further, we also need to look at the areas where our beliefs are based and where they come from. The first source of belief, of course, is our environment. This is something that we can control and that we must actively be aware of. It has been said that of the five people you spend the most time with, you are probably the average of those five people. So, if the relevant five people are positive, vibrant people, who you feel are a force of good in this world, then, in all probability, so are you. Equally if you hang around with five people who are depressive, negative or who continually focus on the wrongs of the world, then likely as not you suffer from the same outlook.

Our environment affects our beliefs from a young age. We learn from our parents, our teachers and we learn in other ways from school friends and our personal experiences. As we grow up we discover that a lot of these beliefs are not necessarily true. As we mature, we question what we have learned and we keep what we agree with and discard or leave behind whatever we no longer agree with. However, we often retain much of the mindset that was learned at a young age. Sometimes we continue to carry some beliefs that we have never questioned, but that destroy our potential. For instance, children who grow up to be involved in gangland killings over drug deals are usually a product of their environment. Their belief system says to them, 'I have got to carry a weapon and I have got to be prepared to use it'. They have this attitude because that is what they have seen and experienced throughout their lives. It is why parents strive to live in better communities and send their children to the best schools, believing that a more supportive environment will give their children a better start in life. People who work in jobs they do not like do so because they have learned from others that change means risk or pain and they have a negative association with it. Well-meaning colleagues might tell them how hard things are in other areas of working life and how lucky they are to have a job.

So look at your environment, because it can impact on your beliefs. If you are not happy with any part of your environment, be it the place that you work, the people you spend most time with, or the things that happen in your home, you need to change that aspect of your environment so that it supports your new beliefs.

Belief and knowledge:

We also develop our belief system from the knowledge that we garner throughout our lives. If we study a certain science, we are tutored to believe that the facts relating to that science are accurate and true. So why is it we no longer believe that the earth is flat or that the Sun orbits the Earth? Science only advances because people ask questions and shake down what is accepted as fact and challenge the thinking of others. Generally, we believe what we read and what we are taught. This has many advantages, of course, in that we can follow in the footsteps of those who have gone before us and learn from their knowledge. We don't have to go to the North Pole to discover that it is cold. We get to understand the basic rules of mathematics because our schools and colleges have put together a system of lessons that allow us to work out basic sums, and continue right up to complicated calculus. This learned knowledge is useful to us if used in the right way. We can learn from books written by authors who lived many years ago, but whose lessons are timeless. Today we can go on to the internet and find answers to questions in an instant. In fact from an information perspective, we are more powerful than the kings of old, who despite all their wealth and their minions, might have had to wait many days or weeks to get information on a particular subject or to discover how their army was faring in a battle in a foreign land. Now with access to the internet, multiple media channels and digital libraries, we have direct knowledge on any subject almost instantly.

This information helps to create our beliefs and enhances our understanding, but we nonetheless need to be watchful that the knowledge that we allow into our lives supports us in being the people we want to become. It is the knowledge that we focus on that becomes our reality; this in turn affects our beliefs. Is there really any merit in knowing on an hourly basis whether the stock market is up or down? Do we need daily updates on wars and the misery they cause? I am not suggesting that you should not be aware of the world around you, but if something major happens, you will find out soon enough. Instead of increasing your knowledge from news channels or water cooler chats with colleagues, you could strengthen your positive beliefs by increasing your knowledge on your area of expertise, becoming more informed about the things that can assist your customers or colleagues. This not only helps others, but is also another way of reinforcing your personal beliefs. When you are informed on what is relevant, it creates a sense of certainty. This knowledge is positive and powerful; it adds another layer of surety in your mind that you and your place in the world are important.

Belief and experience:

Personal Best People: Jez Cox - Performance Coach and Team GB Duathlon manager
"A powerful and effective way to avoid the destructive effect of dwelling on potential negative occurrences is to build a visceral force-field of positive images, which underpin a resilience of spirit. So that as the negative occurrences arise those feelings or thoughts themselves become obscure in your own inner sea of positivity."

The other way we create belief is from experience, the information based on what we have done or what has happened in the past. If you have ever tried to cook a Christmas dinner and ended up eating takeaway after cremating the turkey, your belief system might tell you not to try to cook Christmas dinner again. Equally, if you believe you are a good golfer, for instance, this belief might be based on your ever-improving performance, or on the fact that you consistently beat friends or those you play against in competitions. We can use experiences to either help us or hinder us. We do this by choosing to recall vividly the times when we have succeeded and put out of our minds the times when we fell short. This may sound like borderline narcissism but it is not; it is simply a powerful way of giving ourselves reinforcing reasons as to why we will succeed, and it confirms to you that you are good enough.

Personal Best People: Bernie Siegel - Author and Healer
"One of the best ways to make something happen is to predict it."

Focusing on our success and leaving to one side our less than stellar performances, allows us to create a foundation for seismic change in our beliefs and subsequently our lives. Although our past is not our future, we can still use this reinforcing power to focus on our success and to recall times when we achieved our desired outcomes.

The most powerful way to change your beliefs, particularly when you don't have a frame of reference, is to create in your mind the experience as if it was here now. Just as you might look at a past experience, try to imagine a future experience that you want in the same way. See the images and hear the sounds of this future experience as if it was something that was in your memory and you were recalling it.

The reason for doing this is that your subconscious mind does not differentiate between something experienced in reality and something just vividly imagined. Your mind acts upon the images and events that you think about most. Do you doubt this? Have you ever

224

experienced a vivid dream in which you were being chased? I bet it felt pretty real at the time. Have you ever got choked up when watching a heart-wrenching movie scene? Did you shed a tear? You know movies are make-believe, don't you? We all do, but few of us feel as confident in the sea as we used to, after watching 'Jaws: The Revenge'!

THE GREATEST

In 1975 the reigning world heavyweight boxing champion Muhammad Ali had been unable to agree terms to fight any of the main contenders for the title, and he offered journeyman fighter Chuck Wepner the opportunity to challenge him for the crown. Ali was already a legend by this time, having defeated George Foreman and Joe Frazier in the preceding years. As champion, Ali was guaranteed $1.5 million dollars to defend his title. Wepner would be paid $100,000, substantially less than Ali, but still the biggest pay day of his life and for the first time in his career he would be able to train full-time. The fight was held on March 24th and ex-marine Wepner believed that he could survive anything that Ali threw at him.

When the fight started, it appeared obvious that Ali intended putting on a show. In the early rounds he had the opportunity to take Wepner out but chose not to. He appeared to be toying with his less talented opponent, the supreme athlete dancing around the wildly swinging challenger. The champion and the watching crowd were in for a shock, however, when in the ninth round, Wepner caught Ali with a solid blow to the body and the champ went down. Ali later argued that Wepner had stood on his foot. As the referee started his mandatory count, Wepner went to his corner and apparently said to his manager, "Start the car, we are going to the bank, we are going to be millionaires." Wepner's manager looked behind his protégé and saw Ali rising to his feet. "You better turn around, Chuck," he said. "He is getting up and he looks pissed off." In the remaining rounds of the fight, Ali handed Wepner a boxing lesson, beating him severely and cutting him above both eyes. As the fight drew to a close, Ali also broke the challenger's nose and Wepner, who had hung on gallantly up until then, seemed certain to be stopped. Wepner, despite being bloodied and broken, made it to the last round of the fight. The challenger was well behind on the judges' scorecards when, with only nineteen seconds remaining in the fight, Ali hit him across the temple and sent him crashing to the canvas. Tired and disoriented, Wepner was counted out and Ali had scored another victory, albeit not the easy one that had been expected.

Wepner was not a talented fighter; he was not well conditioned, nor did his record suggest that he would be anything more than target practice for one of history's most renowned boxers. What he had was belief. Belief that he deserved to be in that ring and the belief that he could stand toe to toe with 'The Greatest'.

Wepner received a favourable press for the courage he displayed and the power of his self-belief impacted the TV audience of many millions. This impact was perhaps greatest on one particular viewer who believed that, despite all contrary evidence, one day he could become a movie star.

This out-of-work actor was so inspired by the fight he had just witnessed that he started to write a screenplay based on Wepner's gutsy performance. He wrote the screenplay for the film over three days and nights. He imagined that he would play the role of Wepner and he became so immersed in the project that he took virtually no sleep in the seventy-two hours it took to finish it. His devotion has to be admired. He was approaching his thirtieth birthday and his only claim to fame was to have appeared in one soft-core pornographic film and a couple of other movies in which he had non-speaking roles. By his own admission, he was fairly washed up; he had no job and no income. From time to time, simply to keep his dream alive, he would write screenplays in the hope of selling them to a studio.

At the time he was living in a cramped apartment with his wife. In fact, his abiding memory is that he could both open the door of their tiny bedroom and close the window, while sitting on the bed. Money was tight to the point of being non-existent and things became so bad that he eventually decided to sell his dog. He loved the dog but he was struggling to find money to feed himself, much less his dog, and felt that his pet would have a better quality of life with a new owner who could look after him.

He regularly argued with his wife because he wouldn't take a job. The jobs available were fairly menial, but it wasn't pride that stopped him. His fear was that if he took a job, he would get comfortable, he would become accustomed to a regular pay cheque, and this would take priority. Looking for acting work would become secondary, meaning his hopes of becoming a movie star might never be realised. He knew that by not taking a job, he was making life difficult for himself and his wife, but it was the only way to keep the flame of his dream alive, even though it appeared highly unlikely that he would ever get a breakthrough in his acting career. He was beginning to develop a reputation amongst theatrical agents and representatives throughout New York as someone to avoid. His skills seemed limited and suitable roles were hard to find, but he was relentless, visiting some of the agents several times, on one occasion even sleeping in a representative's office in order to be first in line the following morning.

He was on yet another casting call when he met producers Bob Chartoff and Irwin Winkler. Yet again, he failed to impress with his acting ability and he was turned down for the part. However, on the way out of the door, he mentioned to the two producers that he did a bit of writing. The two men suggested that he might want to drop something off. Down on his luck, he decided to come back with the boxing script that he had been working on. He brought the script to the two men, who were complimentary about it. They felt that America needed a hero story. The mid seventies were a melancholy time for the

United States for this was soon after the Vietnamese War and Nixon's resignation. Winkler and Chartoff saw that an all-American hero might be a tonic that moviegoers would enjoy. The actor was surprised that his screenplay met with such enthusiasm. However, both producers were adamant that if they became involved they would be using a well-known actor for the lead role. They explained to him that he had virtually no acting experience, had never played a lead role and that no one in their right mind would fund a motion picture using an unknown actor as lead. The two producers told him that they would ensure he was well paid for the screenplay and that there had been interest from some of Hollywood's A-listers. At the time Ryan O'Neal, Robert Redford, Burt Reynolds and James Caan were all solid box office draws and were considered for the role.

The actor thought about the offer, but felt that if he did not secure the main part for himself the opportunity might not rise again. Chartoff and Winkler suggested to him that if he took the money for the screenplay, it would give him enough of a buffer to concentrate on his acting and find a breakthrough elsewhere. This was tempting, but he felt that this was the right movie and the right role for him and he tried to convince them that he would be the best person to play the boxer. The two producers adamantly refused; initially they offered him $25,000 for the screenplay. Incredibly, the actor, who at the time had $106 in the bank, declined. Three weeks later, Winkler got in touch again, suggesting that they should meet and discuss the film in more detail. Yet again, the two producers were adamant that he would not play the lead role, but sweetened this pill by offering him $100,000 for his screenplay. The actor silently considered this huge sum of money. He had taken the bus to the meeting because his $40 car had blown up. But yet again, the fact that he would not play the lead role was a deal breaker. He walked away from a $100,000 contract. Three days later he was offered a $120,000 deal. Again, on hearing that he would not be playing the boxer, he refused. In the subsequent weeks, the producers increased their offer, first to $150,000 and then to $175,000. Again they were turned down. Finally after a heated telephone exchange they made what they promised would be their final offer. They were prepared to give him $250,000 for the script and a minor role in the film. The actor considered this monumental amount of money and his current situation. He was living on the breadline in a small cramped apartment, sleeping in a room so small that he could open both the door and the window at the same time. He had no money, he had no car and he had even sold his dog, but he still had belief. He believed that this was his time and if he walked away from it, the chance might never come round again. He told himself that he had handled poverty fairly well and the truth was he did not need much money to live on. He called the men back and declined their offer. They told him they would not be back in touch again.

Weeks passed and the actor decided that he should perhaps see if he could find anyone else who might be prepared to make the film and give him the main role. Unbeknown to him, Chartoff and Winkler were still interested; the movie had now got into their blood and they were convinced it could be a success if it was managed properly. Eventually they decided to appeal to the actor's common sense one last time and met face-to-face with him. At that meeting he was offered $300,000 which was then raised to $330,000 and still there was deadlock over the lead role. Eventually, the two became so exasperated by the amount of time and effort that they had put into trying to get the project going that they agreed to let the actor play the lead. However, far from offering him $330,000, they told him if he insisted on the lead role, they would only pay $35,000 for the screenplay and a percentage of any profit that the film made.

Irwin Winkler and Bob Chartoff were experienced producers. They loved the idea of the movie, but were now convinced it would not be the box office smash they had hoped for and consequently they spent only a million dollars making it, having originally planned a far bigger investment. From this modest budget, the Rocky series of films not only became a multi-million dollar franchise but catapulted the lead actor and writer, Sylvester Stallone, into Hollywood superstardom. The first Rocky movie won an Oscar, as well as a Golden Globe and several other accolades. Stallone's career went from strength to strength and he became the highest-earning actor in Hollywood.

As a postscript to this story, Stallone supposedly went back to New York and stood outside the shop where he had sold his dog to a man who had been buying groceries. He stood outside the store every day in the hope that the man was local and that he would come by

231

again. Eventually, after nearly two weeks, the man and Stallone's much-loved pet came past. Stallone offered the man a multiple of what he paid for the dog but the man refused to sell. Stallone offered $100 and then $500. This was also refused on the grounds that the man and his family had grown to love the dog. After a protracted negotiation, Stallone ended up paying the man $15,000 and giving him a walk-on part in the film Rocky. The dog that Stallone loved so much was Butkus, who also appeared in the movie.

Belief is unlimited power in action. The challenge most of us face before we start any great adventure is that we doubt ourselves. We doubt whether we will succeed, so we lack the conviction to follow through. If you think you are going to fail, you are not going to be committed and you will find it difficult to persevere should you encounter difficulties. However, if you start with a belief system that says this will absolutely work, if you start with a strong enough belief, even when it is not particularly founded on fact or on any level of experience, you will achieve your end. You become excited and energised. You are driven to get up early and to work late. Suddenly everything that you dreamed might be possible in your life becomes possible.

Thinking and belief:

Personal Best People: Brian Bacon - CEO and Chairman of the Oxford Leadership Academy

"Meditate. Begin each day with ten minutes of an inner reflective exercise. Be still in your mind and concentrate your thoughts. Imagine yourself as a spark of light energy. Connect your higher being or your understanding of the Source. This gives you inner peace and power."

Most of our thinking power is non-conscious. By visualising the experiences that you want in your life, you create reinforcing thoughts and beliefs. Research has discovered that thoughts are measurable; they are impulses that fire and control neuron patterns. When you understand this, you realise that taking time to visualise what you want to see in your life is not some air-headed notion. It is a shortcut to achieving what you want. Start using this method now and judge the effect and impact that it has on your life.

Personal Best People: Flemming Bligaard Pederson - CEO Ramboll and European CEO of the Year

"I have achieved my expectations. I have had such ambitions all my life even if I have to admit that many things are different than originally anticipated and the path here has also taken many rounds and bends I had not foreseen but overall the situation is very close to my expectations."

You can experience great things in your life, faster than you could believe. Simply by seeing the result you want in advance, you can create things the way you would like them to be. You are not a bottle on the waves of the sea, you can control your beliefs and the single most important part of this chapter is that you can create unshakeable belief simply by seeing the results in advance; by living them, by getting into the state of mind as if they were already here. Some of the people that I spoke to used this precise tactic to take massive steps forward in their lives. Others articulated it less precisely, but talked of imagining the outcomes that they wanted and of thinking things through. The reason I am such a passionate believer in this, is that it absolutely gets results. You can shortcut years of trial and error simply by seeing the results you want in your mind now and developing an unshakeable conviction that you are going to achieve your goals. Believing that your life will be as you want it to be is almost the elixir of achievement. With belief all the other traits of success fall into line and events come into being. Circumstances that could never have been predicted occur at just the right time. Your personal commitment has to be to develop unconquerable belief in who you are and what you stand for.

Your beliefs create your reality. If you believe nothing else believe that.

PERSONAL BEST POINTS:

Beliefs are shaped by our environment, knowledge and experience.

Environment

• Look at your environment. How do you feel about your home or work place?

• Who are you spending most of your time with?

• Are there any things that you need to change?

Knowledge

• What are you focusing your attention on?

• What are you reading or watching on a daily basis?

• Is this supporting you in being your best?

Experience

• Can you recall times when you performed well?

• Are there times in your life when things just flowed?

- Commit them to memory, remember the state that you were in at the time.

- Are there things that have happened that are stopping you from moving forward or that shook your belief? Can you now recognise these things, understand their lessons and move on?

BE YOUR BEST: Do this. Imagine yourself every day being the person that you want to be. Create a future history for yourself by vividly visualising your desired outcomes. Do this twice a day. Judge on results.

CHAPTER 11: **Emulate**

If I have seen farther than others, it is because I was standing on the shoulders of giants. - Isaac Newton

History shows us that emulating what others have done is a powerful method that individuals and companies can use to grow faster and more effectively. In essence, learning and duplicating the success of others while avoiding their mistakes. Could Barack Obama have made it to the White House without the intelligent advice and support of his wife? Not according to Obama. The philosopher Plato learned at the feet of Socrates. Would we ever have celebrated Monet's work had he not met Eugène Boudin? Howard Schultz, the CEO of Starbucks, publicly credits Warren Bennis for much of what he knows. One of America's prominent industrialists, Charles Schwab, worked for Andrew Carnegie. Jack Welch, the CEO of GE, was close to Scott McNealy, the former chief executive of Sun Microsystems. Richard Branson sought to learn from Sir Freddie Laker. Would the world have ever heard of Eminem if producer Dr Dre had not taken him under his wing? Archimedes mentored Galileo. Mark Antony was a protégé of Julius Caesar. Alexander the Great learned from Aristotle. Whether we call it mentoring, modelling, coaching or emulating, the fact is that the most certain and quickest way to achieve success in any area is to learn from the experience and knowledge of other people who have already done it.

Role models:

Virtually every person I spoke to while researching this book told me that they had a strong role model at some point in their life whether it was a parent, a teacher, someone who gave them their first job or somebody with whom they started a business partnership. They had developed a relationship with someone who was more than their guide, a person who had a deep and lasting influence on their life. The deeper these conversations became, the clearer it was that achievers model themselves on the person or people that they so admired. They actually took on the qualities and experiences of those individuals, by emulating their behaviours and strategies. The clues left by other people, companies and organisations provide us with a roadmap to success. Rather than trying to reinvent the wheel or discover a breakthrough strategy by ourselves, we can use the experience, knowledge and mindset of others to short-circuit the learning process and develop ourselves far more effectively.

Personal Best People: Flemming Bligaard Pederson - CEO Ramboll and European CEO of the Year.

"I have learned from all the people I have met through my life, both from the good and bad sides. I have adapted what I considered to be the positive elements in compliance with my personal fundamental values."

To emulate is to identify the primary thinking, methods, actions and attitudes of people that have achieved results similar to those that we want to achieve.

This does not show a lack of original thought. Duplicating the qualities of successful people and organisations in an intelligent manner is simply a way for us to make our ideas happen more efficiently. Success leaves footprints and whatever has been successfully achieved previously can be achieved again if we follow the same strategies. Patterns can be copied to bring enduring success into our own lives quickly.

Personal Best People: John Redwood - MP
"I was Council house boy from Oxford but I went to America as a young man and saw the wealth created there. When I came back to the UK, I knew that could be done here as well."

How can it be that two people go into the same business and one becomes a phenomenal success and the other does not? Some people from humble backgrounds with no contacts and only a limited education will become hugely successful in life, while others who are born with every available advantage fail to ever attain great heights. Why is this? What are the key differentiators? The primary differences can be found in the thought patterns of successful people. By studying the way that they think, how they process information and how they behave, we can learn to emulate them and achieve success of our own.

THE FIRST APPRENTICE

Today, The Apprentice has become a hit TV show in both the US and the UK, but it was originally the brainchild of British-born TV producer, Mark Burnett who, in 2004, relentlessly pursued Donald Trump to become the face of the show. The show's premise is that a dozen or so budding entrepreneurs compete with each other for the opportunity to join Trump's organisation and learn business skills directly from the billionaire property developer. In the UK, Alan Sugar, now Lord Sugar is the primary judge and taskmaster but the show's concept remains the same and is one that we can all relate to we understand why the apprentices vie for the coveted prize of being mentored by someone who is very successful in business. The show's global success has allowed Mark and his production company to go on to make other reality-based TV programmes, also with worldwide distribution. His successes have included Survivor, The Contender, The Voice and Are you smarter than a ten-year-old?

Mark credits his success to the role models who have influenced him throughout his life, particularly his parents and a man he worked for when he first moved to America. The greatest impact his parents had was that they never criticised him; they told him that he could do anything. No matter how outlandish Mark's ideas were, they told him that he could achieve them. Mark grew up in England and joined the army, experiencing active service in the Falkland Islands before moving to the US. When he arrived in America, he had very little money and was desperate to find employment. A friend tipped him off that a local couple were looking for somebody who could be their chauffeur while also acting as a nanny to their two children. Mark really needed the work, so he called round to see the couple that evening and was able to secure the job based on his army experience. The family were provided with not only the chauffeur and nanny they had wanted but also, given his military background, a security person, all in one. Sometime later Mark moved into a similar role with another couple, looking after their two boys and acting as their driver.

Mark was in awe of his new employer, an entrepreneur called Burt Borman who was also an immigrant, and they remain friends to this day. Borman ran a hugely profitable insurance business and Mark would talk to him about his career and his life in an effort to understand how he had built up such a successful enterprise. Burt told Mark that some of his biggest drivers could have been considered disadvantages. He had started at the very bottom; to Burt this meant that the only direction he could go was up. Burt had no family in America; therefore he had no safety net or back up plan, he had to make the things he planned work out. Another thing that he thought had helped him was that as a recent immigrant, he looked at things from an 'anything is possible' perspective.

Eventually Mark stopped working as Burt's driver and instead became a sales associate in one of his insurance offices. But another piece of advice from Borman was that in order to become really financially successful, Mark would have to go in to business for himself at some point. Burt told him, "Work for yourself, start small and build."

Mark did decide to start his own small business and began by selling T-shirts, part-time on Venice beach. It was here that Mark met Howard Gabe, from whom he rented some fence space that faced the beach. Howard was another person who gave him great guidance. The fence that Mark rented was in a prime spot and cost him $1500 per month. Mark had been able to negotiate a knockdown cost price of $2 per T-shirt from a wholesaler of imperfect items and was selling them for $18 each. He was sure he could make a profit given his only expense other than the T-shirts was the rental of the fence space.

Mark explained his business model to Howard and showed him some of his shirts. "You'll do fine," the older man told him. "Good stuff always sells." Mark made a hesitant start on his first day due to his lack of sales knowledge and his fear of being rejected by passers-by. But things soon turned around and Mark found himself overwhelmed by people wanting to buy his T-shirts; Howard had to come down to help with bagging the goods and taking the money. Mark went home with nearly $1000 that night and over the next two years perfected his sales skills on Venice Beach – the very same skills he says that he used to get his TV shows into production some years later.

We can understand the power of having a strong role model or adviser in our lives, but how do we model excellence? How do we duplicate the thinking patterns and strategies of others? It isn't always as simple as just asking them; often when someone is particularly skilled at something it is second nature to them and they do not always put conscious effort into what they are doing. They are so adept that they just get on and do it; they consequently find it difficult to articulate how they do what they do. Therefore the onus is on us to extrapolate the key strategies that they employ.

Three Keys to Emulation:

There are three primary routes into the minds of those who are successful; three ways to help us copy exactly what they are doing so we can achieve the same result. We have already looked at the first route in the previous chapter. Belief. We need to understand what their belief systems are; not only their belief in themselves, but in the world around them. What do they think? How do they view themselves right now? How do they see themselves in the future? How do they envisage their lives developing?

The second route is their mental processing. How do successful people interpret information? What is their attitude when they receive news, be it good or bad? How do they react when things don't go according to plan? We have already discussed the difference between success and failure and how, if we see failure as feedback, we can never fail. What do successful people say to themselves when they self-talk?

The third route is in their physical energy. Remember that nothing happens without energy and the energy that successful people have is deeper than the energy to simply keep going throughout each day. We need to study their entire physiology. How do they carry themselves? How do they move? How do they communicate? All of this has an impact on their biochemistry.

It may sound simplistic, to say that by simply copying the way someone thinks and moves we can achieve the same success. But duplicating some of their thought processes and behaviours in combination with a strong belief and an effective strategy has been proven to bring about fast results. To understand how someone thinks and behaves requires spending time with them and questioning them. If you find someone that you would like to emulate, but are not in a position to get close to, observe them when possible and find out a much as you can about them. This will help you to understand their methods. Equally we can tap into the mastery of those we have never met or who have long since left this life by reading articles and biographies about them; each piece of information will help us to build a clearer image of their thinking.

Learning is a piece of cake:

In a café close to where I live, the chef makes some of the best cakes I have ever tasted. The café has an open-plan kitchen which is visible from the eating area and I have often watched him make cakes. What interests me is that he tends not to measure out the ingredients. He is able to put the ingredients together without referring to a recipe book or even double-checking that the quantities he is using are correct. There is a parallel in life here. Many of us would look at the chef and say, "What a natural! He is just a talented baker." However, the truth is that he probably makes a cake of some kind every day; it is something he has done over and over again, so he has learned how to put the ingredients together without reference or guidance. If I wanted to make the same cake as the chef, the best thing I could do would be to emulate him exactly.

If I stood opposite him in the kitchen, when he reached for the flour, I would need to stop him and measure out exactly how much flour he put in his bowl and then do the same myself; the same with the sugar and again with the butter. Every time he took an action, or added an ingredient to the mixture, I would need to stop him and again measure exactly what he had done and by doing this I could blend my ingredients in the same way. If I then put my cake in the same oven at the same temperature, our cakes should be similar. Now clearly, it could be argued that with all his years of practice, the chef could finish or ice his cake better than I could mine. However, the truth remains that despite having no previous knowledge, I could bake a very similar cake by emulating the chef's expertise. Continuing the example, if I practised repetitively, I too could bake the same standard of cake without having to measure out or weigh the ingredients. That is the power of emulation.

Personal Best People: Lord James Mackay - Longest Serving Lord Chancellor
"I attribute a lot of my success to the inspiring teachers that I had. They had a profound influence on me."

ICE CREAM AND FOOTBALL

The seaside town of Largs in Ayrshire is famous for its ice cream. It is a quiet, picturesque town, with a large retirement population and well-known as the place where the Vikings first landed in Scotland. What is less well-known is that Largs is home to one of the most powerful forces in world football, a Centre of Excellence built by the Scottish Football Association some years ago. Coaches and prospective managers go there to earn the various licences they require to become qualified professionals. The world-class coaching provided at Largs is headed by their director of development, Jim Fleeting.

After his playing career, which saw him represent clubs such as Norwich City, Tampa Bay Rowdies and Ayr United, Fleeting went into football coaching and management before becoming Head of Football Development for the SFA. The Largs Centre ethos is to provide the very best coaching to those who will go on to coach others. The success of the centre is incontrovertible: its famous alumni includes Sir Alex Ferguson, Jose Mourinho, Craig Brown, Walter Smith, David Moyes, Owen Coyle, Andre Villas-Boas as well as other world-class managers from all over the globe.

Alan Stubbs, former Celtic and Everton defender, initially took his coaching courses in England before being persuaded by a friend that he should go for his A-licence in Scotland. As an experienced player, Stubbs felt that he would have more or less seen it all and heard it all during his playing career. However, when interviewed, he admitted that he had very quickly realised that he did not know as much as he thought he did, and he had been amazed by the amount of time and effort each coach commits to preparing and planning every training session.

As well as being struck by the amount of time that went into planning every session, he realised how naïve he had been as a player, when he would just turn up to sessions, do what the coach asked and then go home again without giving what he had done much thought. However, having now had the benefit of learning from experienced coaches, he gained a full appreciation of what it took to be a top coach and was afforded a much broader picture.

Jim Fleeting and his colleagues at Largs have set a very high standard and it can be no coincidence that at the time of writing, the English Premiership, probably the richest and arguably the most successful football league in the world, has seven managers who were trained in Scotland.

Jim credits this to the cultural backgrounds of those managers as much as to what they learn at Largs, but he does acknowledge that there is a world of difference between on the one hand being a player and on the other being a coach. When speaking about the skills provided to those who take their licences at Largs, Jim said, "As a player you usually complete each session without understanding what you are really doing. If you are told to run to a tree and back, you do it because that is what the coach asked you to do." However, to become a top coach, it is critically important to understand the reason behind every action. The staff at Largs give each prospective manager the insight they need to be technically adept and push them to prove that they are assimilating the knowledge. The final requirement is that each prospective coach must write a near book length report on what they have learned and then present their material. Jim said, "We try to be systematic, we cannot necessarily give them the people skills they need to manage a team, but we can ensure that they are technically competent."

Established managers are regularly invited to present their ideas and strategies to those studying at the centre and, given the number of world class managers who have studied at Largs, it would appear that success feeds success. It is a fine example of emulation in practice, and Jim explains the impact this deep immersion learning model can have by referring to a conversation that he had with former Swedish national manager Lars Laagerback.

Laagerback led the Swedish team to the final stages of five consecutive championships and he did it by focusing on those elements he could influence. As a coach he recognised that the players available to him were not the best in the world. Sweden has a population of less than ten million people and in world football terms has consistently punched above its weight. Laagerback's philosophy was that even though his players were less skilled than their opponents, they could still win by being better in areas outside of ability alone. Consequently he focused on regimented formations, ensuring that every player knew what they should do in a set play. He demanded that every member of the team be as strong and as fit as possible and he maintained discipline at all times. Beating more gifted teams would be hard enough without having a reduced number of men on the field due to a sending off. Laagerback's concentration on these elements meant that for the next decade, Sweden qualified for every major tournament while other countries, larger in terms of population and with a deeper footballing heritage, did not.

If we precisely duplicate the mental and physiological actions of other people, we will get similar results. As with anything in the world, if one person can do it, so can we. How did we learn to talk? How did we learn how to ride a bike? How did we find our way to school? When we first started working, how did we become effective in that role? The way that we did it was by duplicating what others did and modelling their strategies. So, if someone that we admire is doing something outstanding, something that we would like to duplicate, the only question we need to ask is: how are they creating that result? I will always come down to these three things – their beliefs, their mental processing and their physical energy.

Think of someone that you admire right now, someone that you either know personally, or a public figure. What is it that you admire about them? What characteristics do they show? Keep in mind that we don't have to copy every part of a person's personality in order to model the part that makes them successful. We might admire the leadership shown by Winston Churchill but we don't have to smoke cigars to identify his core skills. George Best was a footballing genius but not a paragon of healthy living. If we wanted to become a successful bodybuilder like Arnold Schwarzenegger, we could commit to finding out what his belief systems were in terms of physical development, understanding his training methods and how he managed to find the motivation to continue his daily routine when he felt tired. Further research would reveal his diet and how he carried himself physically. Additionally, we could investigate how he acted in front of his rivals, what he said to them before a competition, how he posed and how he engaged with the judges. By taking on these elements and using them together with an intelligent strategy, we can get a similar result. Will we win Mr Universe? Who knows? But we will reach our potential faster than if we have to try to figure everything out from scratch.

Personal Best People: Sir Frank Williams - Founder Williams Grand Prix
"I learned by my mistakes and if I was being fair and honest I'd say I had very good mentors along the way. Also I must say, operating in Formula 1 you come across some formidable individuals, people who are very clever, who are commercially very astute, Mr Ecclestone is the best example, very clever people and if you have brains yourself you'll learn from them."

Emulating someone is about getting the same or better results by using similar strategies in the area of their expertise. So whether we speak directly to someone we want to role model, or read their biography, or carry out another form of research, we need to understand what drives them. We need to know what their beliefs are, how their mental processing works and how they manage their physical energy. Doing this lets us plug in to their state at any given time.

Personal Best

Your state is simply the emotion that you feel in the moment and defines the way that you experience life. If you want to be happy, you need to be happy inside your head. You could win the lottery tomorrow but if you are a miserable person, the short-term joy you experience from your new riches will soon be lost and you will feel miserable again. Admittedly, you will be rich and miserable which is arguably better than being poor and miserable but you will still be miserable.

You can get into anybody's mind. If you know somebody who seems always to be happy or physically vibrant or financially successful or a tremendous communicator, by doing what they do, you can get the same result. You simply need to control your state.

The United States of You:

Our state is the result of hundreds of thousands of neurological processes that are constantly occurring inside us. Most of us allow our states to simply happen without consciously trying to direct them. We will succeed or fail according to how well we manage not only our states but also our behaviour – which is driven by whatever state we are currently experiencing. We may feel tired, lethargic and depressed or energised, vibrant and happy; these states will affect the decisions that we make and the way in which we interact with other people. State is exactly what we should be looking at when we want to emulate someone.

Do you recall the three key parts in emulating someone's success? They are belief, mental processing and physicality. Our state is also driven by these three elements:

- Our personal belief system – what we believe about others and the world around us; how we think things work.

- Our mental processing – how we represent things internally in our mind, how we mentally picture things, what we say to ourselves, how we interpret events.

- Our physical energy – the way in which we stand, move, and breathe; this is also driven by what we put in to or do to our bodies. The food we eat impacts our physical energy; alcohol, drugs (prescribed or otherwise), sugar and other substances will also affect our biochemistry. Another critical part of how we experience our physical being is the effects of exercise we take (or don't take) to remain healthy.

We can change our state at any time and with immediate effect. So, how do we do this?

Using imagination:

Simply by acting As If. Take the time now to imagine how you would feel if you were the Prime Minister or a global leader and then act as if you are. What would you be thinking? What would your

253

beliefs about yourself be? How would you feel about your country? What would you think about the world at large? Next imagine how you would process that information. What would your understanding of things be? How would you receive bad news? How would you communicate with people? And finally, stand the way you would stand and breathe the way you would breathe if the cameras were on you and you were about to deliver an important speech. Try it. Just imagine how you would feel as the leader of your country and by using your mental and physical resources to achieve this state, hold yourself and behave as though you are this person for the next sixty seconds.

Personal Best People: Ron G Holland - Entrepreneur and Author
"I love working with people. I know what it is like to have a mentor, my mentor helped me turn my life around. So with my clients I not only work with them on business acumen but also the mind power side of things. The ones that embrace both are the ones that really fly."

Here's another. Imagine that you are a professional boxer about to fight for a title you have strived to attain throughout your career. The venue is packed, the noise is incredible, and you are behind your corner men, walking towards the ring. You can hear your entrance anthem playing. You have never felt so strong or prepared in your life; you know you can beat your opponent. Now stand up; how would you be holding yourself? How tense would your muscles be? What would you be thinking? How would you be breathing? How much desire would you be feeling?

You may have been relaxed and sitting comfortably before you acted these roles, but if you have done the exercises effectively, you will now feel differently. That difference is due to a change in your state and shows that we can change from being a passive reader, to a statesman, or to a boxer, in a very short time frame.

What we are thinking can change our heart rate and cause us to have different experiences. How would you act if you felt uncontrollably happy? What would you be saying to yourself? How would you be holding yourself? What would happen to the tension in your face? How big would your smile be? Would you be laughing? This is what state changes can do; they can actually bring about change in our physical bodies and in our minds.

So if we can control these feelings, why wait? When we get depressed or sad or feel let down, we can either allow ourselves to get into a sad state or we can choose to control our state. The greatest control you have over yourself is your physiology, and you can tap into it immediately. By focusing on the best parts of your life and carrying yourself with energy, you can trigger an emotional change to make yourself feel happy.

Take the opportunity and time to model people that you admire. These may be people you know personally or public figures that you see on television. Take some time to research them, listen to what they say during interviews, including the tone and inflection of their voice and how they interact and connect to other people. Do whatever you can to get into their state of mind. Carry yourself as if you are them. It may sound simple, but we tend to overcomplicate solutions. This technique works. As your state controls how you experience life, the states that you spend the most time in are going to define how you experience most of your life. By emulating what successful people do, you can emulate their success in your own life.

Personal Best People: Frank McKinney - Real Estate Rockstar and Bestselling Author
"Learn from highly respected, successful people. Find out what makes them tick. I still remember looking up to people and thinking I could footprint their behaviours."

We can emulate any area that we choose. We can emulate the beliefs that we looked at in the previous chapter and we can emulate the strategies that we are going to look at in the next chapter. By emulating people who have achieved what we want to achieve, we can realise our own goals more quickly.

PERSONAL BEST POINTS:

- Who do you admire and what do you admire about them?

- What characteristics or traits do they show that you could emulate?

- Can you now alter your state by changing what you are thinking and the way in which you are using your physiology?

BE YOUR BEST: Do this. Practise and use the knowledge you now have to positively alter your state by changing your own thoughts and physiology in any given moment to support you in being your best.

CHAPTER 12: **Strategy**

All men can see these tactics whereby I conquer, but what none can see is the strategy out of which victory is evolved. - Sun Tzu

In the previous chapter, we looked at how we can emulate the success of others. In the same way, we can duplicate the strategies of others to create success in our lives. Once we have an effective strategy we can repeat our success over and over again. Strategy is when knowledge and planning come together with action. When we develop intelligent strategies, which deliver fast, efficient results, we can take giant leaps towards the goals we want to achieve in our lives. In order to deploy an effective strategy, you first of all have to be clear on what you want. Consciously or subconsciously, the people I interviewed were clear about the outcomes that they wanted and were driven by that purpose. Being sure about what you want is the cornerstone to building an effective strategy.

Goal-setting:

Setting goals can, on occasion, seem like a tired subject. Read any book on personal achievement, or go to any seminar or effectiveness, and this subject will almost certainly be cited as a fundamental part of what you need to do. There is a reason for this. It works! We can fall into the trap of thinking that we know all of this and that we have heard it all before, but few people set effective goals. The familiarity we have with the subject breeds contempt. We all know that we should set goals, but how many of us actually do it?

When you commit to something, the first part of that commitment is writing it down, committing to what you want in clear terms. Doing this means that not only do you understand it intellectually, but also that you send a strong, clear message to your subconscious mind as to what you want to achieve. We have already looked at the importance of beliefs and how they affect your decision-making. One of the best ways to develop strong beliefs is to create a strong future history. The way that we do that is by being clear about what we want. This is why taking the time to write down clear, concise goals provides absolute clarity regarding your ultimate outcome. When you write your goals down, you stimulate the creative force within you. There are so many stories of people who have done this and found that events turned in their favour almost as if they were tapping into a collective consciousness. The creative force involved in writing goals seems to stimulate forces we are not aware of.

Personal Best People: Brianna Glenn - Team USA World Championship
Long Jumper

"This year I wrote out my goals and made them as specific as possible so that with everything I did I knew exactly why I was doing it and what I was working towards. I had what I called my "desire statement" – the main goal I want to accomplish-- and for a month straight I wrote it down in the morning and at night to make sure it was a part of me and that I had it ingrained in my brain."

Goals and reality:

When you are absolutely precise about what you want, you create a strong link, an associative condition which will drive you and lead you into circumstances and events that you could not have predicted. This may sound a little esoteric for you. Maybe you put such things down to luck or coincidence, but the more people I interviewed whilst putting this book together, the more I became aware of a pattern emerging. The majority of my interviewees were clear about their outcomes. They worked hard with faith that they would achieve their goals – and events just seemed to fall into place. They met people just at the right time and events occurred that seemed inexplicable. In many instances they put it down to happenstance or being in the right place at the right time; they seemed embarrassed to explore the subject too deeply. But crucially a few did, and it became clear that when one is committed and has a clear plan in place, remarkable things seem to happen. Taking the time to set goals achieves real results. It commits you to becoming the person you want to become.

When you are clear about what you want and why you want it, then setting clear, defined goals becomes simple. We can set grand goals for our whole life in terms of the people that we want to be, and the overall achievements we want to attain. We can also set smaller goals, in terms of what we want to achieve in the short term. However, our goals should be congruent – they should relate to each other in the jigsaw of our life.

There is little point in setting a goal of having a lean, toned, healthy body if you also have a goal of being the world's greatest pie eater. The two goals just don't sit well together. So whenever you take the time to set a goal, make sure it aligns with your life's purpose and supports you in where you want to go. As with any goal, if you have a big enough 'why' you will figure out the 'how'. That is how goals become powerful and compelling. So identify what you want in your life and concern yourself with how you will achieve it afterwards. By taking the time to commit to a written goal, you are putting into place the cornerstone of your strategy. You are committing yourself to a compelling future. Simply by having a plan, you allow your subconscious mind to start quietly working towards the achievement of your goal.

When you create a new future for yourself, you commit to another tenet of the Personal Best ethos. If you are committed to change, if you are committed to continuous improvement, then by writing your goal down you are saying right now that your situation isn't perfect, that it needs to improve. You are acknowledging the fact that you could be more, have more or achieve more. In doing this, you put pressure on yourself to become aware of where you are falling short, but this is a positive pressure that allows you to design a new future. This healthy pressure is sometimes described as inspirational dissatisfaction. You become aware of areas where you feel your life could be improved.

What is success?

Ultimately, as we have already seen, success means different things for different people. What one person wants could be the opposite of what somebody else wants. There is no single definition of success for any one of us. But if we try to encapsulate what success means, then probably the easiest way would be to use the word expansion.

Wanting to achieve a certain goal often boils down to the amount of expansion that you want in your life. If you want to become wealthy, then you wish to expand your wealth. If you desire to become more knowledgeable, then you want to be more educated in a certain subject. If you are looking for a wonderful relationship and a life partner, then you want more love in your life. So whatever you want in your life, whatever goal you are setting, you are effectively telling yourself that you want more. That is why when we set goals we have to be careful as to how we define them. For instance, if you wanted to get into great physical shape, your goal should not be focused on losing weight. It should be phrased in terms of expansion. There is a difference in outcomes between people whose goal is to create a lean, healthy body and those who want to get rid of excess weight.

Success is often determined by what we focus on. Focusing on a healthy body opens up the possibility of a better outcome than does focusing on excess weight. To put it another way, when people focus on losing weight, their thinking is polarised on the additional weight rather than the actual outcome they want to see. Your goals are about expansion and you send a message to your subconscious mind regarding what you want more of. If you are endeavouring to lose fat, the last thing you want is more of it. So set this type of goal in terms of having a trim, vibrant, healthy body. This is not simply semantics. If you want money, focus on an abundance of money and not on getting out of poverty. If you want to be healthy, focus on health, not on getting rid of illness.

Be creative:

What would you do if you knew you would succeed? If you knew that whatever you attempted would come to fruition? It is a sad truth that many of us don't try the things that we would love to because we just don't believe that it will happen. We fear rejection or failure, but if you knew that you would succeed, what would you do?

Personal Best People: Indro Mukerjee - CEO Plastic Logic
"You have to look to the future. Twenty five years from now when I am sitting in a home for retired ex-electronics executives. I have to know that my business is still functioning in the industry in which it is involved. You have to have a future plan."

Take the time now to write down what it is that you want in your life. For the next few minutes, I invite you to suspend your disbelief. You do not need to know how you will achieve each goal. All you need is to be inspired enough. If you know what you want and you have a strong enough reason for wanting it, anything is within your reach. Get yourself into a state of belief. Get yourself into a creative state. Develop the feelings of positive expectation. What can you come up with?

Taking the time right now to write down some of the goals that you want to achieve might be one of the most important things you will ever do. So the first set of goals could be 'you' goals. How would you like to improve mentally, physically, as a person? What would you like to learn? How could you contribute? How would you like to be remembered? Whose life could you touch? What skills could you develop? Take the time to get excited about your goals. When doing this, simply brainstorm anything and everything that you would like in your life. Later, as you move through this process, you can prioritise and decide which goals are really important and fundamental to you. For the time being just get excited and become engaged in writing down any and every goal that occurs to you. Write your goals in the present tense as if you had already achieved them. So they read like statements of fact not a wish list.

The big why:

Having done this, now write down why they are important. What will you see in your life if you achieve them? What makes this so compelling? Remember that if you are not coming up with strong enough reasons, you need to either revaluate your 'why' or perhaps you need to aim at another goal. Maybe the ones that you have written down are just not compelling enough. If you have a big enough 'why', relating to any goal, you will figure out the tactics to achieve it, so make sure you have a strong reason for wanting to achieve each outcome. Now do the same with other areas of your life. What about your career? What about the adventures you would like to go on? What about your family? What about your financial goals? Follow the same process. Write them down in the present tense. Each goal statement should read as though it has already been achieved. So you could begin each statement with the words, "I now have," or "I have achieved." Then having done this, get absolutely clear as to why these outcomes are important to you. This clarity brings you closer to realising your achievements.

Personal Best People: Charlotte Bray - Composer
"I do write down my goals. I time-table the work I have confirmed for the future and then I keep a 'wish list' of pieces I would like to write or people that I would like to work with."

Prioritise:

Once you have completed this exercise in all the areas that are important to you – health, wealth, family, career, spiritual and so on, you must next take the time to decide which ones are most important. Perhaps you want to sail around the world solo but you also want to get closer to your children. There is a challenge in achieving both, but life's delays are not life's denials. Your intelligence will tell you that you have to prioritise your goals. Some may be important in the long term and others might feel more urgent and need to be addressed immediately.

Take the time to edit the goals on your list and decide which are the most important, the ones that you are really going to focus on. There are maybe some goals that you want to achieve over the next few weeks or months and others that you want to complete this year. Other objectives may take longer to realise. The process remains the same. Get absolutely clear about the reasons that you want to achieve these outcomes. If you are having difficulty in selecting the most important goals, ask yourself this: if you could have one of these things happen in the next twenty four hours which one would have the biggest impact?

Hardwire your goals:

You can rocket to success by writing your goals down and then, to be absolutely sure of their attainment, you have to condition your internal system. You can condition your neurological pathways to feel the pleasure, significance and joy that attaining these goals will bring you. If you do this, you become emotionally anchored to the experience of achieving each of these goals. As with almost everything we have looked at, the method for this powerful conditioning is very simple. All you need to do is take a ten-minute break two or three times a day to review your goal sheet and imagine what it would be like to achieve these goals. Go through them one by one, closing your eyes and putting yourself in the mental state of having achieved these outcomes. How would it look? How would you feel? What would you be saying to yourself? What would be exciting about it?

Your goals are just part of life's journey. It is an important thing to remember. Success itself is simply a journey. The most empowering thing about achieving your goals is how you develop as a person. If you have a goal to make a million pounds, then it is exciting to think of yourself as a millionaire, but what is even more exciting is that you become the type of person who can create enough value to generate that amount of money.

Putting it together:

So let's recap. You should by now have a list of compelling goals and beside each one, the reason why it is so important to you. What will it give you? How will you feel and what will it generate in your life? You will now also be able to begin the discipline of visualising yourself as if you had achieved each one of these goals. Be sure that you do this at least twice daily.

Once you have these building blocks in place you can take the vital step and take action towards the attainment of each goal. Take action right now. Look at your goal list and pick at least one major outcome that you want to achieve and do something now. Download the information you need from the internet. Pick up the telephone and make an appointment. Whatever you want in life, whatever it is that you want to do, you have to create momentum. This is the second element of strategy – action.

Relentless action:

As I have already pointed out, action speaks louder than words; action speaks louder than everything. Now is the time to start living your dreams. When you commit to specifying your goals, you commit to creating a new future for yourself. The key to achieving your goals will always come down to your commitment. Writing goals down is the first step, but the most powerful part of an effective strategy is taking intelligent action towards what you want. As soon as you set a goal, take an action towards it. Anything at all; take any small action in the direction of your goal and you will begin to develop habits that ensure your success.

Personal Best People: Lord Philip Harris - Chairman Carpetright Plc
"My plan was to have three shops. When I had three I set a goal to have ten, once this was achieved I wanted twenty, then one hundred. If I had started out trying to open five hundred stores it wouldn't have happened. You've got to have targets that you think you can reach."

If you have decided that you want a Porsche, make sure that you go online and download the latest Porsche brochure. If you have decided that you want to get into the best shape of your life, go right now and immediately empty your cupboards of any junk foods that won't support you in being your best. The key to achieving your goals is to create consistent actions towards realising them. Once they are written down, once you have decided what you want, you then need to move towards them and act upon your decision. This is strategy in motion. We looked at action in an earlier chapter. People who achieve great things in their life keep moving forward relentlessly. Their vision is so big that they feel compelled to act upon their convictions to ensure their achievement. These people became experts because they did things repeatedly. A great golfer doesn't become great without swinging his club thousands upon thousands of times in practice. Our goals can be achieved only when we take action towards them.

Consistent action:

A further distinction we have to make is that this action has to be consistent. If you are out of shape and you visit the gym for an hour and then return home and look at yourself in the mirror, you will not notice any change. You took action but you didn't see any reward. Hopefully, our intelligence will tell us that it takes more than a single act. It is consistent action that takes us to where we want to go.

Ever heard the saying – knowledge is power? I disagree. Knowledge alone is not power. Knowledge and consistent action is power. Knowledge alone is only data. We have to back it up with intelligent, consistent acts that bring us closer to what we want. If I gave you next week's winning lottery numbers, but you did not buy a ticket, how powerful would that knowledge be? You had the knowledge but you didn't act upon it.

Action and planning:

As part of employing an intelligent strategy, you now have to put an intelligent plan into place. This doesn't mean that you need to know every detail about what you are going to do or who you are going to speak to, but you should be able to establish a rough plan concerning the resources that you will need. You know who you want to become. You know what you need to do. You are committed to visualising your future twice a day. But what else do you need? Take the time right now to note down what resources would assist you in getting what you want. What people could you do with in your life? Who would it be useful to speak to? Who knows something that would be valuable to you? What would you need to commit in terms of time to achieving your goal? Where will you need to go? Get clear on the commitments that you will need to make and the actions that will be required, in order to achieve what you want.

Personal Best People: Nigel Evans MP - Deputy Speaker House of Commons
"Training is the opposite of hope."

Once you have reviewed your goals and started this planning process, it is critical that you do something every day for the next twenty eight days to achieve your most important outcomes. As well as taking the time to visualise them, you must also take the time to act,

271

to reach out and make a contact, or to find some kind of new insight or even simply to research something. Whatever it is that you need to do or study, do it consistently for the next twenty eight days; no matter how small the act, do something.

For example, suppose you want to learn a new language but haven't yet got all the tools that you need. Just commit yourself to learning one new word a day. That single word in isolation doesn't particularly help you to become an expert in that language but it is still an action which, if done consistently, creates the force of habit. Taking action toward your goals is a habit that you must cultivate. Bear in mind that your actions will only be as strong as the beliefs that support them. That is why having a strong set of compelling beliefs is important in achieving anything that you want in life. You will make your decisions based on the beliefs that you have and these decisions will then drive the actions that you take. These actions become your habits, your life and ultimately your destiny.

Action and decisions:

The decisions that you are making right now, each and every day, will mould you into the person that you are to become. You can look over your life and remember when you made or perhaps failed to make decisions, and with the benefit of hindsight you can see how these mental processes have brought you to this point in your life. Your decisions ultimately determine your destiny. You have to decide who you want to become and take action towards becoming that person. Act from the foundation of unshakeable belief.

In the chapter 'Emulate', we looked at how virtually everyone who had been a great success had a key influencer in their life or had somebody they modelled themselves on. The great thing about using that strategy is that you can save yourself a lot of time and energy by learning from the mistakes and indeed the triumphs of others. High achievers are essentially action oriented people. It is why it is so important that every day you get into the habit of taking some action that moves you towards your goal. For most of us, worrying about doing something usually causes us a lot more problems than the actual act of doing it. Once we take the decision to get started and create some momentum, we often find our worries were misplaced. We discover it is easier to act than it was to worry about carrying out that action. Perversely, inaction actually decreases energy. You can spend your whole day thinking about something and working out what you should do. Sometimes you should just go ahead and do it. Create momentum in your life; talking about action and taking action are two different things. As always, you can create, plan and talk forever but eventually, if you are to make progress, you have to take action.

Power of Networks – None of us alone is as smart as all of us together:

Personal Best People: Sir Tom Farmer - Founder Kwik Fit Group
"Surround yourself with like-minded people. People whose company you enjoy and people that you get on with."

Man went to the moon as a result of the concerted effort and wisdom of a group. Doctors make more accurate diagnoses working in partnership with other doctors than they do alone. Drug smugglers remain more elusive when part of a group than when working individually. Even seemingly autocratic leaders usually have a group of senior advisers or trusted lieutenants around them.

Personal Best People: Ali Lukies - CEO Monitise Plc
"A key part of our plan was to partner with a company who would help us achieve our ends. We didn't just need the money. We needed the intelligence also. We met up with a large company called Morse and did a corporate venturing deal - we effectively acted as a subsidiary for them and as a research and development department. What it meant to our customers immediately was we were no longer a start-up but a part of a three hundred million pound business. It allowed us to go out and sell the vision."

I don't know what your dreams are, but I do know that if you can join with others and leverage the resources of an intelligent group you can get to where you want to go far more effectively. This might be as formal as working in partnership with someone or as informal as joining a networking group to exchange ideas and opportunities.

There is nothing shameful about asking for help or advice. This book only came into being with the help of many people who agreed to meet and contribute their ideas. Wherever we look, we see this in action. Facebook, based on a simple idea for a social network, became the world's fastest growing company. LinkedIn is responsible for introductions and new business deals being done across a spectrum of markets. Advertisers are shunning traditional media and promoting their products through the use of viral videos that spread through word of mouth and online sharing.

The Network Effect:

If ever there was a field of human endeavour in which intelligent, well thought-out strategy is relevant, it is getting elected into public office. Whatever your view of the political class, they are generally excellent strategists. I travelled to Dublin to find out more about the power of strategy in politics after noticing the power of networks in the Irish political system. The people I had arranged to meet were all members of the House of Oireachtas; each member (TD) represented a constituency and collectively they were responsible for the direction of Ireland as a country. I met with Noel Grealish, Maureen O'Sullivan, Luke Flanagan and Finian McGrath and they all had something in common, as well as being strong conviction politicians, they were also all independent members of the Irish Parliament and therefore did not have an affiliation with or the support of any of the major parties. I wanted to examine exactly what strategies they had used to achieve this, as standing as an independent candidate is far more difficult than standing with a Party machine behind you.

Generally speaking, party politics works; it is easier to build critical mass and to garner support based on similar beliefs and consensus. There are ready made teams of activists willing to knock on doors and deliver leaflets. Against both the financial and organisational might of an established political party it seems unlikely that an individual could beat all four of the main parties in any given seat. So what methods did these independent TDs employ, and what techniques did they share which could explain how they were not only elected to Parliament but also re-elected time and time again?

The answer primarily appears to sit within the power of their networks. The four all had different philosophies, views and influences. However, they had all been very active at community level from a relatively young age. They further developed their strategy by reaching out to local community groups. Community organisations rely on volunteer help. One can imagine that the individual volunteers within each of these groups felt as though they had more of a voice by supporting an independent member of parliament than they would supporting someone obliged to follow the party line. Additionally, the people who work as volunteers are passionate about their organisation and ready to do everything they can to help its cause. This gives the independents an army of volunteers who will knock on doors, make calls, cajole friends and even chauffeur voters to the polling stations. This approach of garnering strong local links and of word of mouth promotion helped these Parliamentarians build careers and made their voices heard.

CHARLES WIGODER

The power of a network was reinforced to me when I met with Charles Wigoder, who heads up Telecom Plus PLC, a London based utilities provider. The business trades as Utility Warehouse throughout the UK and gives customers significant savings on their gas, electricity and telecom spend. Wigoder joined the company shortly after it was formed. De-regulation had created an opportunity in the utility markets but the business was struggling to make new sales. At the time Charles felt that the residential market was largely being overlooked, as many providers chased large-spending corporates; this was driven by the fact that the cost of customer acquisition was far more easily recouped from companies with large bills than the smaller returns from consumers. Wigoder believed there a fantastic opportunity to build the business by offering large savings to consumers on their household bills, but the difficulty was finding a sustainable model to attract small users without paying the upfront costs of a national advertising campaign. There was no doubt that they could bring benefits to new customers with their winning offer, the challenge was getting their message out to the market.

To overcome this, the business implemented a multi-level marketing model that Charles knew had worked in other industries in the United States. The company positioned itself as a discount club and recruited self-employed agents, who earned ongoing commission not only on their own sales but also a percentage from the sales of new agents that they recruited into the business. Wigoder told me, "We simply did not have the money to spend on advertising. The beauty of this system meant that the agents quickly built recurring monthly revenue and the business only paid out these monies from income, rather than risking capital on advertising or by other traditional routes to market."

In just under fifteen years, the company signed 450,000 customers by offering them significant savings and combining this with first class service. The business is a virtual provider with no utility infrastructure or outlets and now has thousands of independent distributors, some working full-time, some part-time and others on an ad hoc basis. They come from a variety of walks of life and include business people, students, stay-at-home mothers and retirees. Many earn a significant residual monthly payment from customers they introduced in the past or from having simply recommended the Company's services to friends, family and work colleagues.

Charles has an understanding of his own business and cares deeply for the people who represent it, particularly the agents who work on a self-employed basis. He appreciates the challenges they face and takes a genuine joy in telling the stories of those who approach him at the annual meeting to tell him how the business he has created has helped them. He said, "I have had a few occasions now where people have told me of how they were near bankruptcy or divorce because of financial pressures and how the business has changed their lives. That means more than anything, to know that it is making a difference." The template that the multi-level marketing model offered these agents allowed them to harness the power of an extended network, multiplying their efforts and giving them financial freedom.

Charles is visibly moved when he retells these stories. He is a talented executive, having built up several high growth businesses, but he also appreciates that the company he runs is only as good as the people in it and that each of them has their personal path and goals that they want to achieve. Before I left, Charles demonstrated just how hands-on he is when he persuades me that I too should change my services over to Utility Warehouse and disappears from the room returning with the appropriate paperwork. Within a few moments he has painlessly added to the swelling customer numbers of the business.

Increasingly in this digital age, we see both politics and business being affected by this strength in numbers strategy, a good example being the previously mentioned Facebook, which has now become one of the largest companies in the world. At the time of writing it has completed a multi-billion dollar stock market flotation. Facebook has altered the way we communicate with each other and the way in which we draw our friends' attention to events, causes or to small news stories that are important to us. The power within networks can be found in companies as diverse as Telecom Plus, Amway, Avon and Tupperware where peer-to-peer selling has become the de facto method of distribution. This phenomenon has developed ideas, created cult personalities and launched unsigned music acts into the public consciousness. The key to any strategy or any plan is having a clear vision as to your outcome and in today's digital world, distributing your message, your product or your service has never been easier.

THE MAKING OF A PRESIDENT

During Barack Obama's successful campaign for the White House in 2008, he and his campaign team changed the face of US politics forever. It had always been accepted that anybody making a run for the highest office in the United States has to be well funded by large corporate and individual donations. Barack Obama's fund raising broke all previous records and deliberately avoided using large donations or public campaign funds as its primary source. Instead the campaign focused on raising money from private and individual contributors. By the time of the general election, the campaign had raised close to seven hundred million dollars and after the election, i

continued to receive donations as part of a transition project fund. Obama's campaign also focused on clear, concise sound bites. We can all remember slogans such as 'Change we can believe in' and the chant, 'Yes we can' and, as we looked at in an earlier chapter, 'All fired up!' with his audiences across the country replying "Ready to go!'

Obama's strength was in his communication and use of technology to create a huge network of active supporters. Although not wholly reliant on technology, his campaign was innovative in its use of the internet to rally support and, just as importantly, to make policies known. With the use of Facebook, MySpace and other social media, Obama's campaign was able to target the key 18–30 year old demographic, which is ordinarily apathetic to politics. By placing his policies and speeches on YouTube, Barack Obama was able to give his campaign a one-on-one quality that wider media such a television and radio did not offer. Indeed, the campaign was notable for the way in which people formed themselves into local groups for neighbourhood campaign rallying and social activities such as sign making. Additionally, messages were communicated to users based on their consumption habits and this gave the Democratic Party a way to target voters by tailoring messages relevant to them. Basing his communication on consumer data enabled effective grassroots organisation through local campaign teams. Obama also used an online call tool, which enabled activists to make calls from home on personal laptops rather than having to work in a call centre environment. It is estimated that over a million calls were made on behalf of the Obama campaign in this way.

By comparison, his Republican opponent John McCain used the internet in a relatively limited fashion. This meant that the deep level of organisation and wide base of support that Obama enjoyed was never experienced by John McCain. Although the two parties' use of TV and newspaper media was similar, the key strategic difference between the campaigns was the way the Obama campaign was driven by the network effect of many people each contributing financially or by active support rather than relying on large contributions or centralised support teams. This allowed the Obama team to reach more people, more effectively. His campaign, like the man himself seemed to have more of a youthful vigour and vitality.

Barack Obama became the first African American to be elected President of the United States on 4th November 2008. His campaign had involved speaking at over one thousand events, travelling over 250,000 miles and creating the biggest active support base in US political history. President Obama had an intelligent strategy based on his beliefs; he planned and executed an incredibly successful election campaign. He won fifty-three per cent of the popular vote and scored more total votes than any presidential candidate before him.

Like President Obama, if we have a big enough why, we will find a way. Take a moment when you review your goals and decide what actions you could take tomorrow, small or large, that could assist you in the achievement of your goals. What could you do immediately that would take you towards your goal? You should have your list of goals complete with compelling reasons as to why you want to achieve each and every one of them. Beside each one, commit to an action that you are going to take in the next twenty four hours and create that momentum. Make this a habit. Every week complete these actions and set a new series of actions for the following week.

Whatever your hopes and dreams you are responsible for them. You can expect times that will be difficult or when the effort that you are expending seems as if it is not paying dividends. Everyone I interviewed for this book had a similar experience; it is at these times more than ever that you must push on. If you back up an intelligent plan with massive, relentless action, things happen. Circumstances that you could never have predicted will come to assist you and opportunities will arise. People talk of luck, even when talking of their own success, but luck isn't simply some miracle of fate. Luck is when a motivated, hard-working person meets an opportunity and has the intelligence to grab it. Commit to being someone who sees things through, someone who acts rather than dreams. Become a person who achieves, not someone who laments what could have been. Make big plans, take big actions.

PERSONAL BEST POINTS:

Right now, take the time to list the things you want in your life.

- What do you want?

- Why do you want it?

- What will it give you?

Get creative and write down everything you want in the present tense, and then select the ones that will have the biggest impact when you achieve them.

- What actions are you going to take today in order to build momentum?

- Who could you partner or join with to create a powerful alliance?

BE YOUR BEST: Do this. Commit to reviewing your goals and actions on a daily basis. Start building your network; identify not only who can help you, but just as importantly, who you can help.

CHAPTER 13: **Thinking**

Consciousness succumbs all too easily to the unconscious influences and these are often truer and wiser that our conscious thinking - Carl Jung

In the 2010 movie *Limitless*, the main character played by Bradley Cooper is a down on his luck writer who has been recently dumped by his girlfriend. He lives in a cramped, dirty apartment and is in arrears on his rent. He has no regular income and has spent the advance payment he received from his would-be publisher for a book he has yet to start writing. In the movie, a chance meeting with an old acquaintance ends with him being offered a magic pill. His friend tells him that he is working for a pharmaceutical company which is testing a pill that has not passed any clinical trials, but promises to give users incredible levels of cognitive ability, insight and access to knowledge that lies dormant in their minds. Despite the obvious risks, our hero has little to lose and takes the pill. Everything that was said turns out to be true; it gives him an incredible clarity of mind. He has a heightened sense of awareness, he is able to communicate with people at a deep level and he has fantastic levels of energy and focus. Cooper's character can now recall any piece of information that he has seen, read or heard. He finds his learning curve is dramatically shortened; he learns to play the piano in a week and he completes his long-delayed book in two days. Languages come easily to him, complex algorithms, mathematics, the stock markets are all easily understood. The insights he now has give him a quality of life he could previously only dream about. All of his neurological pathways which he could never previously access, now open up to him.

Limitless is an enjoyable film, but of course it is based on fantasy. Such a pill does not exist. However the energy to access improved states is already available to us and sits within our minds. You have an absolute ability to develop not just your logical thinking but, far more importantly, your automatic consciousness, the power that drives your world.

Personal Best People: Bernie Siegel - Author and Healer
"I act and behave like the person I want to be and rehearse it until I do it and I take from the teachings of the sages of the past. My unconscious creates my future."

Throughout this book we have looked at the traits, beliefs and strategies of high achievers. When embarking on this project my primary agenda was to discover the commonalities between these people. Their backgrounds, career choices and personal lives were markedly different. There were common themes, however, and one o
286

he strongest was something that can be best described as self-trust. It appeared so often that it suggests it could be the foundation of greatness. It's an intuitive core belief. Although driven by different purposes and beliefs, all these people were guided by a deeper consciousness. They spoke of this as an 'inner voice' or 'gut feeling.'

Decisions and intuition:

Charles Haanel was a successful American industrialist who ran several companies based in Missouri the early 1900s. In 1912 he published a series of lessons on personal development and financial success. This resource can be found within the resources section of the website www.personalbest.co.uk and even one hundred years on it is still a terrific examination of the mindset of someone who was well regarded and successful in his field.

In his writings Haanel discussed how we could each tap into the physical manifestation of what was happening in our minds. He wrote about a central point in our bodies which if listened to would guide us when making crucial decisions and act as a great source of intuition. When Haanel wrote about a central point, he meant it literally. He was talking about the point below your sternum at the bottom of your ribcage. If you place your fingers there you feel the point where your solar plexus is located.

Personal Best People: Ron G Holland - Entrepreneur and Author
"I have been teaching people about not thinking for thirty years. Showing
them silence, stillness, solitude and slowing down the brain. The Japanese
have a lovely term called no mind. Where you stop consciously thinking and
allow your subconscious to guide you."

Have you ever made a decision based on gut instinct? Even
when you are talking in metaphors, there is actually a physical
manifestation there. That feeling is what we sometimes refer to as 'gut
feeling', that uneasy feeling when you commit to doing something but
you are not sure you should have. Or alternatively, you feel that
excitement, the adrenaline rush, butterflies in your stomach when you
anticipate something you are looking forward to. Or perhaps a
churning sick feeling when you think you have done something
wrong. How many times have you reflected on a poor decision and
said, 'I knew in my gut that wasn't right'? You are talking literally
when you say that. This intuitive point in our bodies can be used as a
reliable guide when faced with challenges or circumstances we are
unfamiliar with. The issue for most of us is that we do not use it; we
may be aware of it from time to time but we are not sensitive to it
consistently. If we become more aware of this feeling and the way in
which our inner intelligence communicates to us, we can use this
resource to make more balanced, perceptive decisions.

Personal Best People: Alan Edwards - CEO, Outside Organisation PR Advisor to David Bowie, Paul McCartney and Novak Djokovic
"Be alert for ideas and opportunities every waking moment and sometimes even when asleep. Always keep a pen and paper by the bed."

Your inner self:

The act of thinking continuously about something brings it into existence. This ability to tap into your inner intelligence means that you have to stretch your thinking. For some people the discomfort of this type of thinking is such that they dismiss it as bunkum or new ageism. All I ask is that over the next few pages you remain open-minded and draw your own conclusions based on your own inner intelligence. In other words, based on the part of you which intuitively feels something makes sense.

Personal Best People: Brian Bacon - Chairman and CEO Oxford Leadership
"Where your attention goes, your energy flows and life grows."

The entire premise of Personal Best is that this is a self-empowerment book; it provides information that helps you to achieve desirable results. I am at heart a pragmatist. Either something works or it does not; judge this by the results that you get. Commit to using your thinking power at the deepest level and see where it takes you. The act of thinking, of holding the things that you want in your mind continuously, will bring them into your reality far more effectively than any other methodology. The power of thought, laid upon your subconscious, delivers to you everything that you want and need. If that still doesn't sit comfortably with you, you can look at it more clinically, as the power of focus. The things that we place our attention on, the areas we choose to focus on, give meaning to our life; it is how we interpret and understand events. Focus is like a lens on a camera. If your mind is your camera, wherever you point your attention is what you will see. Wherever you direct your thoughts is quite literally what you will see and how you will understand your life.

Perspectives:

Let's imagine you and I went to a party and whilst you were talking to someone, I noticed a couple arguing bitterly before one of them stormed out. Soon afterwards, two guys stood beside me, both clearly the worse for alcohol, and I could hear them plotting how they were going to beat up another partygoer who had in some way offended them. They were intent on delivering a lesson using the reinforcing power of physical pain. I may start to think that this is the type of party I could have done without.

Meantime, you were kicking it with people who were just drunk on life; they were friendly, humorous and insisted you joined them on the dance floor. At the end of the night you exchanged phone numbers with a few people, promising to catch up for a coffee. You thought it was a great party and wouldn't hesitate to accept if you were ever invited back there again.

We had both been to the same party, yet because our focus had been on different things, we have an entirely different perspective of what the party entailed. I would think that it was a fraught gathering with people arguing and plotting violence. You would be juiced, wondering when the next one would be. Our focus dictates the reality of our lives.

Your reality is your thinking:

Renowned neuroscientist Baroness Susan Greenfield spoke to me about the increasing number of people who already take Prozac as an anti-depressive and Paxil to give them confidence. Even children receive Ritalin to help their concentration. Greenfield's concern is that our society is relying more and more on drugs to control our moods and performance. During our conversation she referred to her book, The Private Life of the Brain. In it she discusses the concept of seeing thoughts as verbs. A verb is a doing word, so merely by thinking something, that thought can be brought into existence. Your thoughts are electromagnetic currents running across your brain. They are measurable; they are things. Greenfield contends that the brain is not an unchanging organ but is significantly shaped both by what we do and by our experiences. She is not talking figuratively when she says this. As one of Britain's top neuroscientists she is talking literally. At a microcellular level, the complex network of nerve cells and nerve endings which make up constituent parts of the brain are actually changing in response to stimuli. The brain therefore, is malleable not just when we are children but throughout our lives.

The piano experiment:

Greenfield refers to research conducted at Harvard Medical School when volunteers, who had no previous experience of playing the piano, were split into three groups. The first group took part in intensive piano practice for five days. This meant hours of study each day and included feedback from instructors. The second group was taken into an identical room with an identical piano but they simply sat with the instrument. They did not play it or think about playing it. The third group were taken into the same room and were told not to touch the piano but simply to imagine that they were practising the piano exercises. The results were astonishing. Those who had simply sat in the room unsurprisingly achieved no more success in playing the piano than they had previously. Those who had taken piano lessons and practised showed a marked structural change in the area of the brain associated with dexterity and finger movement. However the third group that simply imagined that they were playing the piano showed improvement which was almost as pronounced as those who had actually received the lessons.

The basketball experiment:

In a similar study carried out a number of years ago, a larger number of students were tested for their skill in shooting a basketball at a hoop from the free throw line. Again the students were split into three groups of equal size and of similar skills in order to make the test as fair as possible. The first group were the control group and for the next few weeks not only did they do no practice, they were not even allowed to go into the gym. The second group went to the gym and practised free throws for twenty minutes daily. The third group were again not allowed to go to the gym, but instead went to a room and for twenty minutes imagined throwing basketballs at a hoop, effectively practising only in their heads, but not physically touching a basketball.

At the end of the testing period, the first group which had not practised either physically or mentally showed no improvement. When retested, their scores were identical to those before the test. The second group who had physically practised shooting real free throws scored twenty-two per cent higher than their earlier effort. The big shock was in group number three who scored twenty per cent better than they had previously – almost as much as the second group, but without having touched a basketball for the entire length of the test.

The results of this research seem counterintuitive, as we tend to believe that we must have the physical practice to overlay on the mentally imagined scenario. However, the subconscious mind cannot tell the difference between real experiences and imagined experiences. So if there is something that you want to improve, one of the ideal ways that you can do it is to imagine yourself and see yourself partaking this new activity. The absolute power of your thinking can bring about improvement beyond what you might believe possible.

Information and reality:

Serious research is now being carried out on how our brains not only process information but also on how they actually affect our reality. The world as we know it may be significantly different from the way in which we perceive it. How would it be if human consciousness could affect the behaviour of particles at a quantum level? What if the laws of science are different from what is generally accepted? Humans in general and scientists in particular have a history of holding on to false beliefs based on interpretations of information that are later proven to be flawed. We regard ourselves as intelligent but for all the barriers we have overcome as a species, we remain mystified by our own consciousness. The mind, body and universe connection has produced countless books, gurus and alternative medicines. Many people, particularly within the sciences and certain professions, do not feel comfortable with this subject matter

Nevertheless, there is no doubt that the emerging sciences of quantum physics and epigenetics are changing our understanding of the link between our thinking and our physical world, challenging current scientific theories and forcing us to look with new eyes at life as we presently know it.

You are more than just the result of a genetically coded strand of DNA. Intuitively, I think you would accept that you have an inner voice, a level of consciousness that is not based on the genes your mother and father gave you. Something goes deeper. Research is now revealing to us that the cells making up our bodies are not predetermined by a genetic code but are dynamic and modified by our environment, and in particular by our emotions. Our thinking quite literally affects us at a cellular level. The significance of this is that we have to change our perspective of being the victims of a predetermined genetic code and understand instead that we are masters of it.

Francis Crick and James Watson are credited with deciphering the complex structure of DNA. Their experiments, while technically accurate, are now being shown to have been taken out of context. The work done by the two was never validated as being the controlling force of life, but their data was made to fit an existing belief in the scientific community. Emerging knowledge now shows us that genes work as a map that is read by the mind rather than being a fixed quantity. The mind tells each cell what it anticipates and the cell then goes into the map (the DNA), thus producing what the mind created.

The traditional beliefs in relation to our cells being completely controlled by the nucleus, is like the thinking of astronomers of old, who believed that the sun revolved around the earth. If you remove the nucleus of a cell in a process called enucleation, the cell does not die. It can live for months, but in time it will decay because it needs to replace proteins vital for its survival. Far from the nucleus being the cell's brain, it could be better described as the cell's reproductive system. It is in fact the membrane surrounding your cells that gives them intelligence. If the membrane is removed from a cell it would become comatose.

Our thinking is what drives a message via our nervous system to the membranes around each of our trillions of cells. The membranes act as conductors, channelling the messages driven by our thinking and emotions. Why is this a big deal? Because it proves that our cells are programmable in a similar way to a computer chip. Our mind (the central processor) drives data to us. We are close to having incontrovertible proof that this inner intelligence affects our experience of life. Combined with a greater understanding of physics at a quantum level, this revelation could give us the keys to a sustained, abundant, self-healing existence. Your thinking along with the intensity of your focus will deliver into your life anything that you want.

The physics of us:

Until the mid 1980s it was generally believed that atoms formed our world and that these were the smallest particles in our universe. This was debunked by the discovery of sub-atomic particles such as quarks and photons. This then led to the revelation that these particles were in fact emitting their own energies, such as x-rays and radiation. We are all made up of these tiny sub-atomic particles. This means that we do not live in a fixed universe and we cannot consider matter and energy to be separate, and new studies are proving that there is a connection between our thoughts and physical matter.

The most recent breakthroughs have occurred with scientists who are studying quantum physics, enabling them to measure and study the laws that apply at an atomic or microcellular level. They are delivering insights on the often unseen power of human thought. This new science is beginning to show us that accepted forms of physics research do not necessarily apply at a quantum level. Research has shown that the position of matter changes on an ongoing basis until someone glances or takes a fixed look at it. This means that the act of looking at something can make it appear or disappear. It is a fundamental premise of quantum theory that by the very act of watching, the observer affects the reality.

In a study at the Weizmann Institute of Science, several highly controlled experiments were conducted showing how a beam of electrons was affected by the act of being observed. This research, headed by Professor Mordehai Heiblum, showed that the simple act of measuring or watching something changed that something. This seems outlandish, doesn't it? It does not seem credible that matter can change its behaviour, depending on whether or not you are looking at it.

To prove the point, the researchers built a small device which was effectively a barrier with two openings; they then sent the electrons towards the barrier. If like me, you think better in pictures go to the resource section of the website www.personalbest.co.uk resources and see the double-slit experiment link. The scientists used a tiny but sophisticated electronic detector that could spot passing electrons without disrupting their pattern, as it was vital for the observation device not to affect the current. The patterns they captured showed that the electrons acted like waves when unobserved but like particles when watched. The act of observation affected their behaviour. Further research by Aaron O'Connell and his colleagues at the University of California, Santa Barbara, showed how a tiny resonating strip of metal could both oscillate and not oscillate at the same time. Again, the very act of observation was what made the difference.

When we talk about quantum mechanics and things being in two places at once, we are referring to sub-atomic particles, which are things we are not normally aware of and do not normally interact with. Proving that larger objects obey the same rules has long been the desired goal of many eminent physicists. However, nothing is straightforward with quantum mechanics. The larger the object, the more easily its quantum state is disrupted by the influences of the world around it. But there is now a school of thought which believes that there is no such thing as objective or universal reality. What you observe and what you focus upon is what you see. Our observations can change our reality.

We have to begin to accept that our thoughts and our intended focus can affect and change not only our personal reality but also the physical world around us, using the measurable force of the nerve energy we produce between synapses. The notion that humans are merely passive observers of their reality does not sit with the new discoveries of quantum science. You are consciously or unconsciously creating the results that you see in your life. When you change the way that you look at things, the things that you look at also change. This is not just a metaphor. This is literal. Your thoughts can change the world and it is the thoughts of yourself and everyone in this world and anyone who has ever been in this world that have made the difference. It is the only thing that has ever made a difference.

Harnessing your thinking power:

So if you have stayed with this thus far and if you can in principle accept that your thinking is a measurable pulse that can affect your world, how can we alter our thinking? This is where the power of positive thought and Personal Best diverge. I am a huge believer in being optimistic and making the best of situations, but being positive about life, while beneficial, will not of itself bring major changes into your life. The reason for this is that when we think premeditated positive thoughts we are appealing to our conscious mind to control events, but as we know at least ninety-five per cent of the time we are reliant on our subconscious to make us function. What is in our subconscious is the essence of who we are. Therein sits both the problem and the solution.

A tale of two minds:

We work with both our conscious and subconscious minds. Our conscious mind allows us to judge, ascertain and evaluate. This part of our mind handles the planning; it makes decisions, it can project forward and reflect backwards, it can process around four thousand bytes of information per second. This sounds impressive until you understand that our subconscious mind processes about four million bytes of data per second. It has to, because it is responsible for our entire cognitive and physical functioning. Our subconscious mind regulates our breathing, organ function, digestion and blood flow; in fact our entire biochemistry. This part of our mind is habitual, as much an integral part of us as a heartbeat.

Crucially, however, our subconscious only works in the present. It only knows now. This is why so many people struggle to change behaviours. They are feeding their minds software (information) that

Personal Best

is incompatible with their central processor (their subconscious mind). Our subconscious mind acts as an autopilot. It is what allows us to drive our cars while singing along to the radio or chatting to a passenger. When we watch a great tennis player such as Roger Federer or Rafael Nadal, we see this in action. Although they are conscious of the act of playing tennis, most of what they do is subconscious. The ball is moving so quickly that they do not have time to measure velocity, spin, angle of trajectory and combine that knowledge with how they must move their feet, set their body and strike the ball for the most effective return shot. They are reliant on their inner intelligence to take them through almost every shot of every rally that they play.

Most of us have experienced the four-stage competence model when we first took driving lessons; we started driving with our conscious minds but now we use our subconscious minds for much of this activity. Initially we are **unconsciously incompetent**. Not only can we not drive but we have no idea how bad we are. We sign up for driving lessons and around this time we become **consciously incompetent**. We still cannot drive, but having kangarooed the car a few times and accidentally accelerated when we meant to brake, we at least understand that we are unskilled. As we learn, we develop our skills to the point where we are **consciously competent.** We can now demonstrate the rudimentary skills required. Although we may have to talk ourselves through each gear change and manoeuvre, we are able to navigate our way through traffic without our instructor having to intervene. Today we are **unconsciously competent**. We can drive while making a mental shopping list, telling the kids in the backseat to behave, eating sweets and predicting the act of crass stupidity that the driver in front of us is about to commit. At this stage we are driving subconsciously; it is so deeply ingrained that it is habitual.

Personal Best People: Mark Allen - six-time World Ironman Champion
"My motivation eventually evolved into being a pursuit of what I would call
personal perfection. That perfection is a state you get into when you just stop
thinking and analysing and judging what is going on and just become the
action of what you are doing. It's the flow or state when time passes in big
chunks without even thinking about it. It's a state of grace where you are
filled with energy and are totally immersed in your task."

Training the subconscious:

In our day-to-day working, we process information almost entirely in our subconscious minds. Therefore most of our decisions are based on what our subconscious believes to be true. Where do our subconscious truths come from? From a variety of sources; parents, teachers, experience, education. Much of this is useful but some of it is less so. From the day we were born right up until about the age of five, we were basically a recording machine. Everything we were told, the things we learned or understood to be true, impacted on us. Our personalities develop primarily before our sixth birthday.

An ongoing child development study by researchers at Otago University in New Zealand shows that by the time children are three years of age, it is possible to predict the traits that will make up their adult personalities. The research, which follows the experience of one thousand children into adulthood, shows that unruly toddlers are more likely to have antisocial and behavioural problems in later years. This study also discovered that well-behaved three-year-olds stay that way as they become adults. The fact that our subconscious mind is the true controller of our lives is often lost in the myriad of well-intended self-help media. You may have tried to make changes in your life yourself and been frustrated when you returned to old behaviours. The reason this happens is because you are using your conscious mind to try to affect the behaviour of your true thinking mind, the subconscious. This is why we see self-sabotage. This is the reason we sometimes do not do the things we know we must. It does not matter what we tell ourselves at the conscious, intellectual level. We have to make it true in our subconscious.

Making the change:

Our conscious mind is capable of abstract and creative thought. It is also able to move backwards and forwards in time as we daydream or make plans. Our subconscious mind thinks literally, which is why our communication with it must be literal and must be in the present. Although it may be seem counter-intuitive to state something as fact when it appears not to be, this is the way in which our subconscious mind understands information. The most profound changes in our life will be experienced by changing our habitual thinking. Our true thinking mind is timeless; it only works in the present. This is why it will respond to specific instructions only, direct statements given in the first person and in the present tense.

As children we asked lots of questions and more often than not took the answers we were given as fact. Sometimes, when we accept what is not fact as universal truth this can be a beautiful thing. Christmas was never quite the same after the reality of Santa dissolved, was it? However, it is entirely appropriate that we question certain things as we grow and gain new knowledge. How many other things were you told as a child that you never questioned and which remain as beliefs now? If you hear that you are smart or that you are stupid, if you are told that you can be anything that you want to be or that you will never amount to anything, these statements for good or bad become a universal truth for you. During our childhood our minds become programmed with attitudes that remain with us forever and due to our young age and lack of experience, this takes place with little or no conscious filtering. The tragedy is that most people carry false beliefs of this type for the remainder of their lives.

Personal Best People: Mark Emalfarb - CEO Dyadic
"My goals are innately understood in my mind"

As adults we question things more. We have a filter through which any new idea has to pass. The filter is made up of our beliefs and if the new idea does not get through, it isn't passed on to our subconscious mind. The challenge with trying to drop conscious thought into your subconscious mind is that we have to get past this filter. How do we do this? We need to act as a child again. It was in this state that you allowed your mind to take facts as they were given and you and intellectually and emotionally accepted them. We need to return to that state to develop a super-consciousness. I am not suggesting you start believing in the tooth fairy again, or recommending that you lead a life of gullibility, but getting yourself into the state of belief and feeding new instructions to your thinking, omnipresent mind can help you experience a new level of living.

You can do this by using the exercises we have covered already, visualising your outcome, seeing yourself where you want to be, but using all of your senses. Do you remember when you were a child? When you played, you performed as though you were really in the moment. When you scored a goal, you could hear the crowd, you ran with your arms aloft, you probably did the commentary too. If you played with dolls or action figures, you were in the minds of these toys. You moved them, you talked to them, and thought what they would think. This is not some optimistic hypothesis. Doing this allows you to access the deepest levels of your consciousness.

The three-step process towards super consciousness:

This technique is increasingly being used in sports psychology. The most visible example is in winter sports such as bobsleigh or luge. The athletes in these events can often be seen before the start, standing with their eyes closed, moving their bodies as they visualise every turn and bump of the course. They feel the muscle tension as they round a corner, they are aware of the air rushing past them, they hear their breathing. They do not imagine it in the future – they are experiencing it in the present. This is the path to super-consciousness, and it needs to be judged by its results.

Personal Best People: Dave Scott - six time Iron Man World Champion and first inductee to Iron Man Hall Of Fame
"There's no question, the component that is lagging behind is the mental component. We haven't done a very good job of integrating psychology into training programs."

There is a three step process which will close the gap between where you are and where you want to be. Use this GAP acronym to easily remember the steps; the first is letting go of what is happening in your day and becoming Gratefully Relaxed; the second is programming your subconscious mind through Active Meditation; and the third is Perpetual Focus. To ensure effective results, find

306

somewhere you will not be disturbed, and sit quietly for a minute. First of all you have to become . . .

. . . Gratefully Relaxed. This means not only releasing the tension in your body but also becoming grateful for everything you have. We are all so busy that we often lose sight of how blessed we are. The shelter, food and relationships we enjoy are not experienced by all. When we become tense we forget all that we have. When we do this we are telling our subconscious that we do not have enough, that things are not as they should be. Our literal, deep thinking mind delivers up more of these experiences to us. The less gratitude we have, the less we experience things to become grateful about. So say thank you. As you sit, breathe deeply, breathe in to the count of four, hold for the count of four and breathe out to the count of eight. As you do this, become aware of every part of your body, relax the muscles in your face and then your shoulders, breathe in to the count of four again, hold for the count of four and breathe out to the count of eight and keep following this process. As you breathe, feel the tension leave your shoulders, back, arms and legs, all the way down to your feet. As you become more relaxed say thank you. Think of the things you are grateful for; your health, energy, family, money, possessions, the love you feel, the experiences you have had and continue to have. If you are doing this correctly you will begin to smile. Once you feel completely free from the happenings of your day, it's time to fire your deep thinking with . . .

...**Active Meditation**. The simplicity of this is incredible. You do not have to write anything down or remember any archaic ritual. Just imagine yourself being where you want to be. Feel what you would be feeling, repeat over to yourself what you would be saying and convert it to the present tense. Feel the muscle tension that you would feel as if you were in the moment living that dream. Be aware of the point in your sternum; allow the feeling of energy and excitement to build there. See it, hear what you would be hearing, develop the feeling of joy, just as if you had realised your goal. Really feel this; it is to the very deepest thinking part of you that you are delivering this message. That is why Active Meditation works, when you feel joyful, abundant, healthy or wealthy, this is what your subconscious believes to be true. This is the way to bring these things into your reality.

Finally we can use **Perpetual Focus**. Live your life as far as possible in a deep thinking, focused state; consistently keep in mind what is important to you. Be aware of the time you are spending. Is it the highest and best use of your time? Whenever you get off track or lose sight of your goals, call yourself to heel with a quick reminder statement of who you are and what you are achieving. This simply means keeping watch over the focus of your mind. It can be hugely useful to keep pictures or reminders of your future in your home or office, placed prominently where you will see them – on the fridge door, on your computer monitor and the dashboard of your car. Even your underwear drawer gets a visit once a day.

Using this GAP system will bring momentum towards attaining our goals into your life quickly and effectively. This method, although not articulated explicitly by the people I interviewed, was delivered to me piece by piece as I came to understand the thinking and methods of those that have achieved success, and I began to see how best to replicate their thinking. The GAP system affects your thinking at the deepest level and becomes your intent.

Intent is a powerful word; it suggests an unremitting commitment to an action or purpose. If I had to encapsulate the most important quality shown in those that I interviewed while writing this book, intent would be the word I would use. Quite simply the power of their intention pushed them beyond what one could reasonably have expected them to achieve. It is perhaps too poetic to call it destiny, but the determination and focus on their goal, the power of their purpose, delivered remarkable results. The intent with which they lived their lives manifested itself in their reality.

Personal Best People: Baroness Susan Greenfield – Neuroscientist
"All I know is sometimes circumstances happen and I go with them and good things happen."

One of the great challenges in putting this book together was developing an understanding of the unsaid. People who enjoy success in their chosen field focus on the primary traits they believe supported

them in their journey. We can learn from these lessons and replicat
this success. However, what we have to acknowledge is that people
even when being completely open and honest about what has made
difference in their lives, will not always be able to articulate thei
subconscious mental processing After all, to do so they would need t
be the subject and the observer of their lives. This is a difficult thing t
do, even if one felt motivated to try. Consequently we need t
understand that each of these individuals has an inner voice
something that intuitively guides them when they are unsure of a se
of circumstances or lack relevant experience in a particular area. Thi
inner voice, combined with the power of their intent, is what make
the ultimate difference. It is what drives their thinking at the deepes
possible level. Within each of them, their subconscious pilots ther
towards the things that they feel they have to achieve and tha
somehow they know they will achieve. This is the most profoun
knowledge that I learned. It appeared time and time again in th
interviews that I conducted; it showed itself in the countless book
papers and programmes that I researched.

The final piece of the jigsaw rests with you and your thinking
Your inner thinking will be reflected in your outer world.

PERSONAL BEST POINTS:

Whatever you choose to focus on is what will dictate your reality.

Your subconscious mind is timeless. It thinks only in the present and accepts literal instructions.

You can re-programme your thinking by accessing your deepest levels of consciousness through the GAP system and using all of your senses to 'see' your desired outcomes in advance.

BE YOUR BEST: Do this. Use the GAP method at least twice a day.

Make this an intrinsic part of your daily routine. Commit to this practice with intensity and judge the results for yourself.

CHAPTER 14: **Being Your Bes**

Do not go where the path may lead, go instead where there is no path and leave a trail. - Ralph Waldo Emerson

The story of your life is being written right now: what ha happened to you, good or bad is in the past and you know by now tha your past does not equal your future. How will the next chapter read What about the one after that? In life you can be an example or warning. Which one are you going to be? When you look back on th narrative of your life, when you look at your story, how will it read Will you have achieved all the things that you thought you could have will you have contributed meaningfully? What will your legacy be?

Using the strategies outlined in this book, you can make hug changes to all areas of your life. This stuff just works! But it is not magic formula in and of itself. You are responsible. You have to tak the necessary actions. Now is the time to make the decision to hol yourself to a higher standard to strive to be the person that you hav the potential to be. Not just for your own sake but also for the other that you could impact and influence.

We have come a long way together and I respect the investment of your time. It is the most precious resource any of us have and we must all use it sagely. Given that you have spent the time understanding the thinking of the achievers featured in this book, I trust that you will put the lessons to use. One of the reasons I wanted to share the message of the success of so many people is that I intuitively felt that the secrets – if they can be called that – of their success would be similar. The same traits, habits and characteristics showed up time and time again. This I hope is the difference that Personal Best gives you: it is about you becoming the very best you can personally be. In a world of gurus, quasi-leaders and soothsayers, the truth is that the only person you should follow is yourself. Just as all the people I interviewed did. Use your inner, intuitive intelligence to harness your own self-mastery and become your highest possible self, in the workplace, at home and in life.

Together we have looked at how critical it is to define your major purpose in life and the importance of having a clear understanding of what you really want to achieve and why you must achieve it. You should know what you want to see in your life and the reasons why this is a must have rather than simply a wish. We have looked at the key traits of enthusiasm, resilience and nerve and how having the passion, strength and courage to realise your dreams means that ultimately anything that you want or desire can be attained. We have discovered that if we focus on our area of specialisation and commit to ongoing, never-ending improvement, we can experience an exponential increase in personal growth and in the contribution we car make to others. We have also looked at how true leadership flow: from personal integrity, the ability to set and hold ourselves to a higher standard and how asking ourselves intelligent, empowering question: enables us to reach beyond our perceived limits.

In the second part of Personal Best we discovered how critical i: is to manage and control our beliefs and how by emulating the winning strategies of others we can take years off our learning curve In the chapter on strategy we looked in more detail at why it is so vita to set empowering goals, and the importance of following through with immediate action. In the last chapter we looked at how our thinking quite literally shapes our experience of life, and the unlimited power of our subconscious minds.

Personal Best People: Tony Hsieh - CEO Zappos
"I think true success is when you get to the point where if you were to lose everything you have and had to start all over, you would truly be okay with it."

Within this book you have discovered not only the key traits o successful people but also the tools that you can use to achieve the same results as they have. Learning from those that have gone before you is like standing on the shoulders of giants; you have insights wisdom and perspectives from people who have realised significan uccess in their chosen field and who, in most cases, have struggled hrough adversity and delays in order to get there.

Innovation and progress come from those who are willing to ccept risk and attempt to achieve things that they have not done)efore. Your personal success will be measured not from what you did vhen circumstances were right or when things were familiar, but from he actions that you took when times were challenging and you were)utside your comfort zone.

In your own way you have the opportunity to impact the world. You can choose to live a remarkable life, to be daring, to be different. You do not have to live a life based on what you know or what is :xpected of you. More than anything I hope that this is what Personal 3est shows; anyone can be extraordinary. By holding yourself to a iigher standard, by maintaining a strong sense of personal integrity in he form of self-leadership, you can design an incredible life. There ire enough cynics and nay sayers in the world already. You can be omething different – an example of what can be achieved.

Desire:

If you have compelling reasons to achieve your goals, backed up vith unshakeable belief that whatever happens you will achieve your nds, then you are already well on your way. You will develop an

unconquerable desire that will deliver you to the shores of you
personal success.

To be your Personal Best, to achieve everything you are capabl
of and more, will come down to how much you want it. This is wh
the power of purpose backed up with belief is so important. If you ar
clear on your outcomes, if you have huge, compelling, driving reason
to achieve these outcomes and if you have massive belief, the rest i
virtually academic. One way or another, the people I interviewed fo
this book had a burning desire; they each had their own magnificen
obsession, a clear goal and a big why, a reason why their target was
must and not a should, and they had the faith that they would achiev
their goals.

Desire is reached sometimes through inspiration, when yo
absolutely feel driven to do something or through desperation whe
you feel the need to make immediate change. Either way it is powerfu
– it can carry you through doubts and uncertainty and beyond th
point of your perceived limitations.

THE SECRET OF SUCCESS

The Greek philosopher Socrates was approached by a youn
man who wanted to know the secret to success. Socrates told th
student to meet him near the river the next morning. They met an
Socrates asked the young man to walk with him along the river. Afte

ome time Socrates suggested they cool themselves by wading into the
vater and carrying on their conversation. The young man agreed and
'ocrates continued the consultation as they both stood waist deep in
he river. Suddenly Socrates grabbed the student and ducked him into
he water. The younger man struggled to get out but Socrates was
trong and kept him there until he started gulping in water. The young
nan desperately tried to free himself but could not break the master's
old on him.

Just as the student felt that he was at his end, Socrates pulled his
ead out of the water and the young man gasped several deep breaths
f lifesaving air. When his breathing had returned to normal Socrates
sked him: "What did you want the most when you were under
vater?" The boy replied: "Air." Socrates said: "That is the secret to
uccess. When you want success as badly as you wanted the air, then
ou will get it. There is no other secret."

Personal fulfilment:

You are the captain of your ship, the master of your fate. The
nowledge that comes from the distilled wisdom of hundreds of
chievers is in your hands. The immense power from the minds of
ome of the best thinkers in the world sits with you. The only question
s: will you use it? Will you commit to answering the questions within
his book, will you take the time to write and review the most
mportant outcomes that you want to see in your life? The more you

draw on the guidance from those that have gone before you, the mor
you will be able to increase your understanding of and ability to us
these methods. How much can you do? How far can you go? Hov
many lives can you touch?

Personal Best People: Frank Mckinney - Real Estate Rockstar and Bestselling Author

"Inspiration can wear off, but aspiration keeps you going. Ask yourself wha do you aspire to be."

Right now you are blessed. The sun rises for you. The win
blows through the trees for you. Birds sing and beauty surrounds you
Take the time to reflect on all of the wonderful things in your life an
in the world around you. Who do you love? Who loves you? What i
great about your life? What makes you happy?

Now it is your turn to fill the canvas of your life with whateve
you want to see in it. If you have read this book through it may b
because you want to give more of yourself. I believe all of us feel a
though we could be better than our current performance suggests o
that we could achieve things that might seem beyond our reach. B
committing to becoming a little better every day, by developing you
understanding or honing your skills, you can not only make changes i
your own life, but also help and positively contribute to the lives o

others. You can do that now. You can start making changes today, rather than someday. I hope you recognise how unique you are, how your individual ability is important not just in achieving your personal goals but also how you could use your skills to help those around you.

Personal Best People: Shama Kabani - CEO Marketing Zen

'Life is unexpected. And, the only thing we take with us when we leave is our deeds and our lessons."

The life you can create for yourself and the people you can help as you make the journey might be one of the most profound and defining experiences of your life. The success you will feel will be multiplied if you can involve others either by helping them out, or by guiding someone, or by sharing your success with those in your network. This connectivity is omnipresent in our lives; sharing our knowledge without the expectation of favour or reward is the way in which we can most impact the world. Giving something, whether it is time, money, your experience or knowledge just seems to attract good things back to you. Why did the people who had achieved so much agree to be interviewed for this book? There was no financial gain for them. It cost them time. They probably had to answer questions that they have been asked innumerable times already in their lives. But each had a spirit of generosity, a desire to share their knowledge with the readers of this book. You. It just seems to be that this is how nature works. The more you give without expecting anything in return, the more good things will flow back to you. The interviewees I spoke with agreed that on many occasions when they had helped somebody, that at some point, somewhere, somehow, someone unexpectedly popped up in their life and returned the favour.

Personal Best People: Brad Feld - CEO Foundry Group
"I have a deep intrinsic motivation, discipline to get things done, and a belief that you only get one chance at life. I also have a strong give before you get mentality – I do many things without any expectation of getting something back for them."

When you help someone not only do you get the feeling of wellbeing from having had a positive impact, but you also increase your own understanding of the matter at hand. To reinforce our learning it can be useful to teach what we know. When you help others, you leave a small legacy; when you make a difference to someone, you remain in their hearts and minds. There can be no greater fulfilment than to know you have made a positive difference in the world. This is why I am such a fan of the Buy1GIVE1 concept that Paul Dunn, Masami Sato and their team have built. If every time something good happened to you or you made a sale or completed a transaction, how good would it be to know that someone, somewhere in the world had also benefited as a result?

So now, my friend, it is over to you. I am not a guru. I still mess up and get it wrong! But I am still learning and with each distinction I make myself closer to the person I know I can become. The same is true of you and when you start to become the person that you believe you can be, you will discover a whole new set of vistas in front of you, new things you can learn, new ways you can contribute. I think every single person that I interviewed in the course of writing this book agreed that success is not a destination; it is an ongoing journey of self-discovery. Realise now, that even when you achieve all the things that you want to, you will have grown so much, understand so much more and be so excited by the sense of achievement that you will be compelled to do more, to find new paths and scale new mountains.

Ultimately in life getting the things that you want will not of itself make you happy. The thing that will give you satisfaction, contentment and happiness is the growth that you will experience in becoming the person that you want to be. Your growth, the increases in personal power that you will experience, how you help and serve others and how you contribute are the things that will define how you will feel about your achievements.

I hope that you will commit to building a life of abundance, based on your purpose and passion. I know that if you do, all the things that you want will appear in your life. As you take action, as you write your story, please share it with those close to you and with a wider audience. Not only will you feel inspired, you can inspire others. So if I can ask one thing from you it is that you share you Personal Best story as you progress, email me anytime barry@personalbest.co.uk or go the website www.personalbest.co.uk add your comments and share your experiences with others committe to being their best.

I urge you to take action, if you want to be your Personal Bes now is the time to start the race of your life.

Every morning in Africa, a gazelle wakes up. It knows it mus outrun the fastest lion or it will be killed. Every morning in Africa, lion wakes up. It knows it must run faster than the slowest gazelle, o it will starve. It doesn't matter whether you're a gazelle or a lion when the sun comes up, you'd better be running.

African Proverb

It's time you made a start. I wish you love, life and laughte Stay in touch. Be your Best.

The Next Step:

Thank you for your time and commitment in reading this book. I hope that the message has been of value to you.

I am keen to engage and to stay in touch wherever your journey takes you.

What is your next move? What are you going to do? Are you going to start a business? Improve your current business? Move to a new country? Change careers? Find your perfect partner?

Whatever you do, please let me know – drop me a line arry@personalbest.co.uk I like hearing from likeminded people and would love to know your plans for the future.

Day to day I still consult with businesses and the people within them, so if you are looking to take your organisation or personal development to the next level, get in touch and let's see how we can work together.

I also partner with consultants who can complement what Personal Best does. So, if you have an area of expertise which you think might fit, or if you think your clients might benefit from Personal Best, let me know and let's see what we can achieve.

Other plans in the near future include new Personal Best books taking the best knowledge on a variety of subjects and delivering titles that give readers insights and strategies from experts in business personal development, health, fitness, life skills and wealth creation.

If you think that you could help co-author a Personal Best book or contribute in some way contact team@personalbest.co.uk

Finally, a favour to ask, if you believe this book could benefit others and you are a Kindle user please click all the way to the last page, where you will be invited to leave a review or share on Twitter and Facebook. Equally, if you are reading this on good old fashioned paper, please feel free to get in touch with your feedback and/or leave a review on Amazon, your thoughts are appreciated and I am truly grateful for any support you can offer in sharing the message.

Barry Duddy

Acknowledgements:

My thanks go to those close to me who have helped and supported during the writing of this book, in particular my brother Paul Duddy, my dear Mum and Lisa.

I also owe a debt of gratitude to those who took an interest, read chapters in work and who helped pull it all together; many thanks to Stephen Cashmore, Ben Galley, David Gordon, Derek Fullarton, Tom Slider, Wes Linden, John Geates, Anne Walker, Stephen Walker and Tim McGuigan.

Equally, a big thanks to the management and business professionals who took the time to look at sample chapters; Lee Shorten, Paul Green, Stuart Blyth, Gordon Cowan, Gloria Murray, Graham Bunting, Stuart MacDonald, Rob Cornish, Colin Millar, Russell Dalgleish, Hansa Pankhania, Mark Wright, Kelly Munro, Alan Dick, Sinclair Gair, John Benson, and Susan Smith. Thanks also to those who show their best week in week out, my friends; Kevin Bloy, John Strachan, Gillian Geates, Lynsey Cooper, Laura Wallace, Alex Dunlop and Laurence Baker.

These people and the others that you will find at www.personalbest.co.uk/team not only help check work in progress, but also brainstorm new ideas, promotions and books. We are always looking to bring more people into the Personal Best family, who are creative, enthusiastic and keen to share their ideas and thoughts. Email team@personalbest.co.uk to get involved.

Personal Best Partners:

Personal Best has developed a strong network that provides services and offerings to those looking to develop their personal, professional and business skills.

Many of these providers will often give free consultations, advice or special offers to Personal Best readers, get in touch and find out how you could work with them.

Find out more by visiting: www.personalbest.co.uk/partners

Buy1GIVE1

Additionally I would invite you to visit Buy1GIVE1 at the following link: www.personalbest.co.uk/b1g1

There, you will find the names of the individuals and companies that support the Buy1GIVE1 movement. Using their services, means that not only do you engage with some of the brightest minds available, but you also contribute to those most in need, simply by transacting with them.

"This may sound too simple, but is great in consequence. Unt one is committed, there is hesitancy, the chance to draw back, alway ineffectiveness. Concerning all acts of initiative (and creation), there i one elementary truth the ignorance of which kills countless ideas an splendid plans: that the moment one definitely commits oneself, the providence moves too. A whole stream of events issues from th decision, raising in one's favour all manner of unforeseen incident meetings and material assistance, which no man could have dream would have come his way. I learned a deep respect for one of Goethe' couplets:

Whatever you can do or dream you can, begin it.

Boldness has genius, power and magic in it!"

W.H. MURRAY

The Scottish Himalayan Expedition 195

Lightning Source UK Ltd.
Milton Keynes UK
UKOW050606200213

206518UK00001B/1/P